MW01600269

WHATEVER IT TAKES

The Unwavering Faith and Miraculous Journeys of Elijah and Elisha

Ardyce Miller-Templeman

Nazkine TV Publishing LLC

This book is dedicated to my husband, Rev. Earl Templeman, who went to meet Jesus April 3, 2023. He was my encourager and strongly supported me in the writing of this book.

CONTENTS

PREAMBLE

It was early morning when Elijah stepped through his tent opening into a pleasant morning atmosphere. The sun was barely peeking over the horizon, promising blue skies along with rapidly rising temperatures. As the sun began its' slow march across the almost cloudless sky, Elijah stretched and yawned. This early morning hour was still cool, and sleep had been sweet and way too short. But he was up and just about awake.

As his brain began to activate, Elijah reflected on how precious these beginning hours were each day. He treasured the moment when he could step through the opening to seek his favorite spot at the base of the closest mountain slope. It was peaceful there. This was where he would sit, reflect, listen, and talk with God. It was also the most beautiful of gifts to his senses just to watch the sun as it at first barely peered over the horizon to begin lighting the world with its bright coloring of the sky.

As beautiful as the sky and as colorful as the clouds which began their day touched by the rising sun, and as comfortable as the weather was touching his skin... while he began his trek to his hallowed spot; Elijah's mind was restless and troubled. He tried to silence these troubled thoughts. He was troubled... very troubled, creating a trembling in his spirit. And it all had to do with King Ahab, the king of Israel. Ahab had continued the wicked practices of previous kings that had led the nation of Israel into the evil practices of idol worship. And God was agitating the spirit inside of Elijah into doing something about it.

With a sigh of frustration Elijah left his humble home and headed into the rocky terrain of the rugged mountain just beyond his tent. Behind him he heard his mother and family preparing breakfast. Elijah was way too inwardly disturbed to eat. He had to once and for all settle this conflicting, agitating spirit within him.

DANGEROUS MISSION

Ahab, king of Israel, was quite pleased with himself. Life was good. His palace was everything he could wish for. He had money, prestige, servants, and slaves in abundance. He enjoyed bountiful food with which to indulge. Then there was Jezebel, his beautiful wife. When he married her, she took the country and his personal life by storm. Could anything, or anyone, have it any better? He was a lucky man. Yes, indeed! He sat back in his chair well pleased with himself and his lavish good fortune. What could ever go wrong? He was, after all, the king.

While King Ahab was busy preening and enjoying his prestige and prosperity he was blissfully unaware that about 100 miles southeast of his palace God was troubling the spirt of a man who was about to make his life very miserable.

* * *

Elijah sat cross legged on the ground, his back resting against a large red, sandstone boulder. It wasn't the most comfortable of positions, but it was private, and it shielded him from the building heat. And Elijah needed quiet: Because he was being confronted with a difficult assignment. Unfortunately, this assignment could mean the loss of his head. And Elijah was partial to his head as he needed it for survival. But Elijah was no coward. Sitting there, back resting against that large boulder, watching the sun continue to rise in the early morning while enjoying a warm breeze softly touching his skin; he tuned his ears listening to the early morning birds. The Blackstart bird intrigued him as it darted in and out of the crevice of a rock a short way from where Elijah sat. The bird was blissfully satisfying a breakfast craving for crawling insects. "God is so magnificent and marvelous in all of his creation," Elijah mused.

With a sigh of surrender to that inner

voice, Elijah finally roused himself and began the walk from his mountain solitude back to his family's place of encampment. He would eat some breakfast, wrap some cheese and bread into a bundle, fill a goat skin bag with water, and head into the direction of that invisible, but very real finger of God.

* * *

The nation of Israel had suffered a succession of very bad kings. Through the warnings of some very brave, and very godly prophets these kings had been warned over and over that God would judge them unless they gave up those blasphemous foreign gods and turned back to Him. Disobedience, they had been warned, would lead to great calamity which was guaranteed to befall both king and people. But the warnings fell on deaf ears. The kings made pacts and treaties with wicked nations. The people worshipped the gods of these nations and engaged in other idolatrous practices. God was greatly displeased and had gone as far as he could allow it to continue. These wicked kings who tried to marry both the Hebrew God with the gods of other lands, were creating the harsh reality that no nation can ever rise above its' leadership. And so, the people engaged in immorality, pagan practices, and forgot the God of their fathers.

Because they worshipped other gods' immorality and lawlessness reigned. The land was corrupt. There were few restraints and so the people lived wildly, their senses insatiable. They worshipped nature, believing that the world was god: Pantheism. Children were no longer revered, as they would too often be offered up in sacrifice to idols. There was the altering of truth, no absolute truth. Words would be redefined. God had warned them over and over. Therefore, he tapped the brave prophet Elijah on the shoulder. It was time!

* * *

King Ahab had grown up in the palace of his father, King Omri who had established Jezreel as his capital and had built an elaborate palace with intricately carved ivory. Then King Omri died, and Ahab had ascended the throne as king. And Ahab wanted nothing to do with these meddlesome prophets. Life was good. Food was plentiful. Jezebel was beautiful and saw to it that all his little whims were taken care of and wants met. His palace was a place of exquisite beauty and comfort. Best of all, he was now the king of Israel. His pride knew no bounds. And in following the practices of his predecessors in making treaties with the kings of the godless nations surrounding Israel, he married beautiful Jezebel, the daughter of Ethbaal, who was king of the Sidonians. Sadly, King Ahab, king of Israel, began to serve Baal, the god of the Sidonians. So it was that God tapped his faithful servant, Elijah, on the shoulder one beautiful morning as Elijah relaxed, resting against that large boulder and directed his attention toward Samaria and the palace of the wicked, offending king.

❊ ❊ ❊

It was in the early part of the month of October when Elijah began his long trek toward Jezreel and the palace of King Ahab. Elijah's mind was in a whirl of thoughts and possibilities of what he would encounter once he arrived at the king's palace. Nevertheless, as he continued his journey he felt a quiet sense of confidence. The God of Israel would be with him, of that he was confident.

It had been a dry summer, as it always was. Fortunately, for this traveler, it was no longer the searing heat of the summer season, but the early start of October. There had been no rain for six months, from April to now October. And the seasonal rains of October and November were about to begin. As he walked that long journey, his mind would focus on the confrontation ahead of him, then upon the land around him. He loved this land: This land of many different contrasts. He was headed toward the Jezreel Valley, a collective term for the Jezreel Valley and the Valley of Megiddo. This valley lay between the Mt. Carmel ridge toward the south and the Nazareth ridge on the north. Elijah was headed toward the city of Jezreel, located in the center of this valley which rose about two hundred feet above the plain on the lower northwestern edge of the Mt. Gilboa ridge. Obedient to that pointing finger of God, he headed straight toward the palace of King Ahab. But he wasn't in any major hurry to reach that palace. He needed time to pray and receive direction in his prayers. So, as he journeyed along Elijah enjoyed the magnificent lay of the land. Anemones, wildflowers of many different varieties, the lilies of the field, all spread in front of and around him. The sight was almost intoxicating in its luxurious spread of beauty. He enjoyed and relaxed in the refreshing springs and brooks along the way. At times Elijah would stand still, or just sit to enjoy the sight and sweet perfume of God's abundant provision through nature. At other times he would bask in the delight of the creatures frolicking in this delightful land spread out all around him. Every so often a fox would cross his vision in search of a meal. He saw deer in abundance. Gazelles played in the distance. Once he spied an Ibex. Then there were the wild goats, leaping, simply enjoying their freedom and life. What an incredible, beautiful world. What a creative God to arrange such an awesome display of His glory.

But Elijah could neither sit nor rest forever in this land of beauty and delight. He was a man on a mission and that mission remained a burning fire inside of him.

This burning fire within Elijah's breast, led him to intercede for both king and people as he journeyed these many miles. As he walked, he would talk with God, pleading with him to spare his people. He knew it would take a major crisis to get their attention. So, he began to earnestly pray that God would stop the rains for three years and six months (James 5:17-18). Maybe then, the people would turn from their idolatrous ways.

✻   ✻   ✻

The rolling hills of the landscape was now changing, and Elijah knew before too long, he would have to face the wicked king, Ahab. Elijah was not about to back down from the call of God; nevertheless, his heart was beating a wild staccato inside his chest.

Gazing into the distance Elijah had his first glimpse of the glittering ivory walls of the palace. The sight was everything he had been told. It was enormous, gleaming in the sunlight. The time was now and he had a job to do. Wearily he pressed on. The journey had been long. Elijah was tired and now he had a ferocious king to locate who could order his head to be removed from his body: Or maybe, Elijah mused, he would be thrown into a very dark and terrible dungeon. It was a moment of awful possibilities, and he was afraid one of those awful possibilities could become that proverbial moment of truth. But now his job was to locate King Ahab.

Elijah found the king walking alone in a field just outside his palace. It was as though God had arranged this meeting in a more private secure setting than inside the palace walls, which suited Elijah just fine. As he approached the king, he began to feel an arising greater sense of emboldenment and confidence that God was indeed with him. The closer he drew to the king the greater the power and presence of God settled upon and through him.

Ahab glanced up to see a man approaching boldly in his direction. This man appeared to be a rather rough/tough fearless soul with fire burning in his eyes. This was no polished prophet who approached Ahab. Elijah walked straight to the king, looked squarely into his face, and declared, "There will be neither dew nor rain in Israel for the next few years except at my word." Then Elijah turned and quickly walked away and out of sight.

The astonished king was so stunned that he had no words of response to this abrupt declaration. Neither could he move as he watched this prophet turn and walk back the way he had come. King Ahab had no idea where Elijah had come from nor where he was going. It was a surreal moment.

* * *

Elijah had delivered his message and now the voice of God spoke into his consciousness. "Elijah, well done. Now, turn eastward and head toward the Kerith Ravine." The Keith Ravine was located just east of the Jordan. "I want you to hide there. You can drink from the brook and I have already ordered the ravens to feed you. "Ravens? Had he really heard correctly? God had ordered RAVENS to feed him.

Elijah had already traveled several days to give his brief message to the king, and his body needed rest... lots of rest... and now he had to turn and head east toward the wild terrain of the Keith Ravine, a distance of about 25 miles. Because it was already later in an afternoon, he figured the trip would take until tomorrow afternoon. Obediently, Elijah turned eastward toward Gilead. By the middle of the next day Elijah entered the wilderness area where he would be sheltered during the early days of the drought that would soon befall the land. With a sigh of relief, Elijah descended into the ravine. The Kerith Ravine was really a wadi with a bubbling, rushing brook racing over and around rocks and stones. The water was clear and cold and the hungry, thirsty Elijah drank until his thirst was fully slaked. Then he found enough soft foliage, made himself a nest and laid down for his first truly restful sleep-in days.

The warm sun trickling between the trees overhead and the soft breeze touching his sleeping form, provided that restful atmosphere Elijah so desperately needed. Late in the afternoon he was awakened by the cawing of a large bird. Coming to a sleepy awakening Elijah noticed a raven standing on the ground beside him. In its' beak was a piece of cooked meat which the bird dropped the moment Elijah's eyes were opened. Landing beside the first bird another raven opened his beak and dropped a piece of fresh bread beside the meat. Then they fluttered away together.

A surprised and grateful Elijah reached out his hand and picked up the offered food. God really had said the ravens had been ordered to feed him while he was here! Was there ever greater proof of God's call upon his life? With a sense of the divine presence and of a humility of purpose, Elijah ate and was full. Then he crouched on the bank beside the brook and again drank to his fill. He was still weary and laid back down in his comfortable nest where he slept the late afternoon and night hours away.

Ahab stood staring after the departing figure of Elijah wondering what had just happened. Finally, he shook himself, headed into the palace where he went on a search for his wife, Jezebel. She always knew what to do. After listening to her bewildered and agitated husband, Jezebel waved her jeweled fingers and armful of clanking bracelets and declared; "Why are you standing here talking to me? You have an army. You have soldiers under your command. Find this man and have him killed!"

Days went by. Then weeks went by. The rains didn't come. Grass began to dry up for lack of water. The daily early morning dew no longer produced moisture. No one had seen this prophet, Elijah, neither did they know where to find him. It was as though he had suddenly appeared out of the atmosphere and then disappeared from off the face of the earth.

October rolled off the calendar. November took its' place. Still no rain. Still no dew Ahab was becoming greatly alarmed. Armies searched while

Ahab raged. One man! One man created this mess and Ahab intended to find him and make him pay for this atrocity.

* * *

LIFE IN THE WADI

While King Ahab ranted and raved, and Queen Jezebel beseeched her worthless idols; Elijah was enjoying a unique camping experience. The wildness and beauty of the ravine was rest and renewal for his soul, and pure delight for all his senses.

After the first bewildering days of being led into the ravine, Elijah settled down to enjoy his temporary new home. The temperature was moderate and there was an abundance to see and enjoy in this private sanctuary. Twice a day, morning, and evening. he would hear a fluttering of wings and several large black birds would come to a landing beside him. They would drop off their offerings, lift their massive wings and take off again. The amazement of God's creativity in feeding him never wore off. This twice daily food supply was sufficient and pure joy.

Along with the food supply provided by the ravens he found a tree of late producing figs. The tree should have been fruit bearing a month ago. Fortunately, this tree, having grown by the water source provided some sweet treats. All in all, the raven offerings, snacks from the fig tree and the cleanest, clearest water to be found anywhere, was nourishment fit for any king.

Elijah enjoyed walking along the wadi. During his walks he delighted in the different foliage to be found: the box-like balm of Gilead, the olive trees that grew along the banks... and flowers... the wild lilies that grew in abundance alongside the brook, along with an assortment of other wildflowers created a delightful scene of beauty. Every so often a fox would materialize, on the hunt for a meal. But the animal he enjoyed watching the most was the Hyrax, a rock badger. The Hyrax resembles an overgrown guinea pig which hides among the rocks and every so often will peek out at the world. Elijah never grew weary watching their curious faces peeking around rocks to observe him as well as the rest of the world surrounding them.

And then there were the wild goats. The wild goats were a constant source of entertainment. They leaped from rock to rock, playing, climbing, jumping, finding joy in just being alive. Occasionally, an Ibex appeared at the water's edge. Even a Jackal could be seen every so often. This wildlife would keep their distance, but none of them seemed afraid of Elijah. He was accepted as part of the landscape.

✳ ✳ ✳

Weeks passed. Months passed. The land became more and more dry and dusty. Crops dried up. Cattle were becoming desperate for grazing and for water. And still the rains refused to fall. In the Kerith Ravine, the rushing, bubbling brook began to dwindle until very little water remained between the banks. Elijah had by now spent some precious months alone with the God of creation who was also leading, directing, providing for his needs, and who one cool morning quietly instructed his servant to leave this place and "go at once to Zarephath and stay there. I have commanded a widow in that place to supply you with food."

Elijah had virtually nothing to pack for his trip to Zarephath. Immediately he climbed the bank and turned northeast toward the city of Zarephath, a Phoenician city sitting on the western coast of the Mediterranean Sea. This journey would consist of about a daunting one-hundred-mile trip well into Greek territory. Interestingly, Elijah was heading into territory not too distant from Jezebel's home city of Sidon.

After close to a year of quietude in the Kerith Ravine, Elijah was well rested, renewed, and ready for the next phase of his adventure. Once again, he appreciated the land as he traversed toward his destination.

Elijah was accustomed to traveling up and over and down rocky, mountainous terrain. The difference this time was the dryness of the terrain. Seldom did he see any little pockets of water. However, he never went without this necessity. Just as God had provided food for the ravens to transport to Elijah, now he saw to it that the hundred-mile journey to Zarephath provided enough pockets of precious water for his servant to drink. Elijah would drink from the clear, pure pockets of life-giving water and then fill his goatskin bag. God also saw to Elijah's need for food sustenance. Elijah would come upon small encampments of nomads who would invite him to eat with them. Other times he would find berries along his way. The God of provision was still faithfully caring for his beloved servant.

As Elijah walked mile after mile toward his destination, he was seeing the beginning results of the prophecy he had spoken against King Ahab. The dryness of the land was startling. Foliage was dry; leaves on plants and trees were not only dry but curling up and brittle. Wildflowers had died or were in process of dying. There were some desert flowers still in bloom, but the entire landscape was becoming a dry barren land. Here and there he saw animal bones bleaching in the unrelenting sun. It was a distressing, sobering sight.

One morning Elijah stood on a rise of ground gazing eastward and saw the bright blue waters of the Mediterranean. His incredible next phase of venture was about to begin. He continued to stand still, studying the waters off in the distance and wondering how God was going to pull this off. Widows were usually the neediest people in the land. But, if God could provide prepared food for Elijah through the transportation of Ravens, he could certainly provide enough for this next venture.

AN EVIL LEGACY

King Ahab was in a foul mood. The entire world was drying up and blowing away and it was the result of one man's brief appearance; the fault of a rough/tough disgusting apparition in the field outside the palace, and Ahab wanted to find him, wring his neck, then disengage it from the man's body... only the man had poof... disappeared. Ahab's soldiers had not located him. Scouts had been sent into neighboring kingdoms. The man had simply disappeared into thin air, as though he never really existed.

The nagging question was, "what to do?" From one end of the kingdom to another, cattle were losing weight, ribs protruding, and all the while these tormented cattle bawled pitifully for water and for vegetation. The sound of their suffering was horrifying to hear. Herdsmen searched far and wide for any patch of green vegetation with which to feed these cattle. Crops weren't producing. So the king of Israel sat disconsolate on a hard rock, pondering, with no answers to give his nation, nor any answers to give his own household. No longer was he gloating over his abundance and lavish good fortune. He was troubled, upset, and could find no way out of this conundrum.

So, Ahab sat, and thought and reflected. His thoughts went to his father, Omri. He remembered the day his father became king of Israel. It had been a glorious day filled with fanfare and celebrations that lasted for a week. The warrior, Zimri had killed Elah, the drunken king who had sat on the throne in the town of Tirzah. Zimri wanted the throne for himself, so he had eliminated the king and declared himself to be king. But the army had another idea. Omri, Ahab's father, was the army commander and at this time the army was engaged in a battle, besieging the city of Gibbethon. They declared Omri to be the rightful king. The army withdrew from Gibbethon and headed to Tirzah where Zimri had reigned for a self-adulating seven days. Now, a frightened Zimri quickly realizing no one would come to his defense, fled into the innermost part of the palace, and set it on fire, burning up not only the palace but himself with it.

A victorious Omri was placed on the throne along with a great deal of fanfare and Ahab rose from the son of a warrior to now the prince of the nation. It was a heady rise of status. To round out his status, his father, Omri had died and now Ahab sat on his father's throne. But the bubble had burst and here he sat on an unwieldy rock with nothing but dried up and dead foliage spread out in all directions, dying cattle bawling off in the distance, water becoming increasingly more difficult to find, and an entire kingdom demanding answers. Being king was turning out to be a tough job.

Sadly, as Ahab pondered this terrible situation his nation was in, he refused to look inward, into his own heart. From one reign to another, the nation of Israel had been led astray into the worship of other gods. It was true they, recognized that Yahweh was the God of Israel and Judah, but as the years passed, they added to their list more and more of the gods of the nations around them, adding them on to their worship of

Yahweh. And the succession of kings continued to lead them further into this disgusting idolatrous parade of evil worship and immoral reveling and drunkenness. Jeroboam was a prime example of an evil king. His son, Noab inherited his father's throne. He reigned two years before he was assassinated by Baasha who copied the lifestyles of his predecessors, after his death his son, Elah ascended the throne. However, Elah would rather party than lead. Arza, his prime minister, was just as corrupt as the king, and together they would drink until they couldn't walk down a hallway without holding onto walls or onto servants. The people finally had a bellyful of the king's excesses. King Bash's army official, Zimri, assassinated King Elah after only two years of reign and stole the throne. Zimri reigned only seven days and burned down the palace, and himself along with it, before he could be captured by the army for his treachery.

King Ahab thought back to the days when Israel and Judah were separated into two kingdoms. Judah had a history of righteous kings, while Israel flaunted their evil practices in front of Israel's many different prophets who warned of what would happen to their kings and to the nation itself if they continued in their wicked ways. After the separation of the two kingdoms, the kings of Israel never bothered to learn why Judah remained stable while Israel rocked and reeled with instability. The reason was simple but remained elusive from Israel's kings: The nation of Judah chose not to fall into pride through carelessness. Their good king Asa had determined to bring glory to the Lord. They would seek the Lord for wisdom, and then to obey and to trust Him. And in times of impeding danger, they would find their strength in Him.

That rock was unyielding and uncomfortable. Ahab shifted his weight trying to find a more comfortable indentation. He was in no hurry to return to the palace as he continued his reflections.

A twinge of conscience pierced Ahab's soul, a painful gentle warning of the consequences that would happen if he and his people didn't return to Yahweh and cast off all these foreign gods. Fast on the heels of that thought arose a vivid picture of his beautiful Jezebel and just as quickly, he uttered a violent curse, hardened his heart against these reflective thoughts and stood to his feet. What did Yahweh have to do with anything? The appearance of that ridiculous vision was only the mutterings of a deranged apparition.

Little did Ahab know, but judgement had already fallen upon him and his nation. As severe as the draught was, they were to soon experience how real and terrible was the one and only true God.

✽ ✽ ✽

King Ahab headed toward the palace: His thoughts and musings still in a jumble. Hard as he tried, he couldn't shake the many stories he had been told during his growing up years. He had sat spellbound at the feet of Jonathan, an ancient wise man who helped maintain the grounds of the palace. In the evenings the boy, Ahab, would often find Jonathan and would listen until night was falling and he would have to return to the palace. Jonathan would tell about Abraham and Isaac, the promised son; about Joseph, whose brothers sold him into slavery, then how he had risen to the second in command in Egypt, saving Egypt along with his own family from starvation during a seven year draught; about Moses leading a rebellious people through the wilderness to the promised land; and about Joshua and the walls of Jericho. He would hear about his ancestor, David, who had been King and how he was a man after God's heart. Jonathan would point out that God was a jealous God and would bless the man who worshipped Him, and Him only. He shared the story of Solomon, David's son who asked for wisdom. Solomon, Jonathan told young Ahab, became the wisest man who ever lived. Then, Jonathan sadly revealed, Solomon kept making alliances with the kings around him, married their daughters, and these women turned Solomon's heart from the true God, and he began worshipping the gods of these wives and his heart turned from the true God to the idolatrous gods of those other nations. "Guard your, heart, Ahab", Jonathan would warn. "Guard your heart. Never forget the true God and worship him only."

But as Ahab grew older and made friends with other young men, his heart grew cold and the culture around him drew a snare about his heart until he partook of the evil practices of these gods…, the temple prostitutions, the groves of Astaroth where sexual raveling's would titillate all the senses: the excesses… all contributed to a growing coldness in the young man's heart. And the God who led his people out of the wilderness, who broke down the walls of Jericho, the God who sat David on the throne, and gave him wealth and the hearts of his nation; this God, the creator of the heavens and the earth, took a back seat, and was scarcely acknowledged.

And now, his queen, Jezebel, was determined to wipe out the worship of Yahweh. Baal was the Phoenician fertility god who sent rain and bountiful crops. The rites connected with Baal's worship were unspeakably immoral. And Ahab, who had been taught about the true God the one who sent the rain and sun and caused the earth to grow bountiful harvests, was ignored. Ahab entered wholeheartedly into these idolatrous practices and had even built a private temple for Jezebel where she could worship, taking part in sexual orgies. Her plan was to exterminate the worshippers of Jehovah and have all the people of Israel serving Baal. And so, she had ordered all of the worshippers of Jehovah to be put to death.

While Ahab headed slowly and with a troubled heart toward the palace; Elijah was gazing into the distance catching glimpses of the Mediterranean Sea. God was directing him into the next phase of his great adventure.

A SURPRISED WIDOW

Elijah stood gazing off into the direction of the bright blue waters of the Mediterranean Sea. The sun sparkling off the waters after the dryness of the dried and brittle desert he had just trekked through, made the scene exceedingly inviting. Now, Elijah turned onto the public road that ran along the seashore and along the spur of the mountain which divided the plain of Tyre from that of Sidon. The city of Zarephath was located about eight and a half miles south of Sidon and fourteen miles north of Tyre. Elijah still had a little way to go before arriving at the city gates, but the cooling waters of the Mediterranean were a feast for the eyes, and the breeze off the waters was a welcome relief from the desert stillness.

Zarephath was an interesting city, noted for its industry. First, the city had two major promontories, each forming an excellent harbor. One was the site of a Roman quay from which they could load the merchandise provided by the city's industry and unload supplies needed for the manufacturing of the industry, products, as well as grain and other needed food supplies. The second harbor was used in the shipments of Phoenician Iron.

Zarephath was a very busy, and influential city. It was a center for pottery production. It produced an abundance of olive oil. It was also a center for metallurgy and was well known for its studies into the properties, productions and purifications of various metals, such as iron and bronze. Zarephath also was a center for the manufacturing of purple dyes. All in all, Elijah was to soon experience a huge noisy, busy change from the quiet year he had been hiding inside the Kerith Ravine along with the stillness of a lonely desert, to this noisy, bustling urban metropolitan area.

Soon, Elijah approached the city gates where his next adventure was about to begin. Just as he entered through the gates leading into the city, he noticed a careworn widow lady engaged in gathering a few sticks from the ground just inside the gate. Elijah felt an inner nudging to approach her. She was so intent on finding these few sticks that she didn't notice Elijah slowly approaching. As he came alongside of the woman, he cleared his throat and said, "pardon me. Would you be willing to bring me a cup of water? I am very thirsty." As she turned and began walking away to get it, Elijah called out to her, "and bring me a morsal of bread."

With that the woman turned back to Elijah and walking up to within a few feet from him, in a trembling voice said, "I do not have any bread, nor do I have more than just a handful of flour and a small amount of oil in a jar. If you will notice I am gathering a few sticks to take home to prepare two small cakes… one for me and one for my small son. We will each have one cake and then we shall die. I have nothing more."

Interesting enough, Elijah knew instantly this was the widow lady God had prepared to bless and to care for him. And he also knew exactly what he was to tell her. "Don't be afraid, "Elijah told her, "Go and do as you have planned; but first, bring me a cake. Then go back and bake a cake for yourself and one for your son. For this is what the Lord God of Israel says, 'the bin of flour shall not be used up, nor shall the jar of oil run dry until the day the Lord sends rain on the earth."

A tiny flicker of hope crept into the hurting, fearful heart of this poor widow as she turned to leave Elijah and to go back home. Doing as Elijah had said to do, she made him a cake of bread. After baking it she noticed with amazement that neither the flour nor the oil had decreased in volume within their containers. Could he really have spoken truth? Did the Lord God of Israel speak through this dusty, man who was still waiting at the city gate? And did the Lord God of Israel care about an insignificant poor widow and a small little boy? Taking the hand of her son the bewildered, woman, who only a very short time ago had lost all hope, took this small cake of bread along with a cup of water and hurried back to the city gate where Elijah was waiting.

As the woman handed him the water and the bread she timidly ventured to inquire where he intended to find lodging. It was obvious by his clothing and speech that he was from Israel. "As yet I have not found lodging," was his reply. In true cultural hospitality she said to him, "then come home with me. I have an upper room in the house where you can stay."

Now Elijah was even more certain this was the woman God had intended to take care of him. Amazed at God's unlimited provisions, Elijah followed the woman and her curious son home. It was a very small humble home. She had very little in the way of possessions, but it was clean. The tiny upper room above the rest of the house was sparsely furnished yet appearing to be comfortable. After a year camped beside the brook in the Kerith Ravine and the lengthy walk across the arid desert, the bed was agonizingly inviting. Elijah thought he might fall asleep on his feet if he didn't get there quickly. However, as the widow descended the staircase the young child continued to stand in the doorway staring at this interesting stranger. Elijah asked the child, "what is your name?" The boy finally found his voice. "Yada" "How old are you, Yada?" "Four", was the one-word response. "Elijah asked the boy if he was hungry. The boy enthusiastically nodded his head up and down. "Yada, your mother is baking a cake for you to eat right now. With a burst of energy, the child was down the steps eager for food while with a sigh of fatigue and deep relief, Elijah was on the bed and asleep before Yada even reached the bottom step.

* * *

Throughout that region the drought deepened while cattle and people alike struggled for daily survival. Still the worshippers of the false gods refused to acknowledge the one true God. They beseeched their worthless idols, poured out offerings from their meager food stores, offered up their precious children to these evil idols, and made wild promises. But the drought only progressed in its intensity. Ahab gnashed his teeth in rage and frustration over the elusive Elijah while Jezebel increased her orgies to her favorite idol, Baal... a Baal that was impotent to make the rain fall and bring an end to the suffering of the people.

* * *

Meanwhile, Elijah waited to hear from the Lord. Days went by, then weeks, then months. Almost two years were to go by as Elijah continued to wait, always marveling how God had hid him in the midst of this city of Baal worship, only eight and a half miles from Sidon, Jezebel's home town. God had placed him for safety right in the middle of enemy territory.!

Elijah would take walks in the cool of the day waiting to hear the voice of God. During the daytime hours he would pitch in to help Yada and his mother Melqart. He gathered wood for cooking, would find odd jobs to help cover the expenses and work of the household. He would frequently take Yada outside to take walks with him, and sometimes to occupy him in play. Elijah learned to love this energetic, happy little child. And that same energetic and happy little boy quickly learned to love Elijah. Then one day tragedy struck. Yada had been sick for several days. Elijah and Melqart were very concerned. The child was too pale and way too listless. A week went by, then very early one morning before the sun had even risen in the sky Melqart showed up in Elijah's doorway, angry, crying and screaming out, "why are you here, oh man of Israel's God. Did you come to me to only reveal how wicked I have been? Did you come to bring me condemnation for all my sins? Alarmed, without even a reply, Elijah leaped to his feet and hurried down the steps with Melqart to where Yada lay motionless, his skin waxy in appearance. Elijah put his hand over Yada's pale lips. There was no breath. He glanced at his chest. There was no movement. Grief stricken he picked up the small body and climbed up to his own room, while Melqart collapsed on the floor wailing in her anguish and pain.

Trembling, Elijah laid the light body on his own bed. Then he stretched himself out across the child's body all the while crying out, "Oh Lord, my God, why have you killed this widow's son: this widow with whom I have found lodging? She has been good to me. She has given me a place of safety while I wait upon you. Now, please, I pray, allow this boy's soul to return back to him." The Lord heard the cry and desperation of Elijah's anguished prayer. The prophet felt a slight movement of the child's body under his own. He dropped to his knees beside the boy where incredulous he watched slight movements of the child, then his eyes popped open and gazed upon this kind, godly man he loved so much. The boy's soul had returned to him, just as Elijah had asked! A jubilant Elijah snatched the child up in his arms and hurried down the steps. Melqart looked up at the racket descending the steps and saw

Yada snuggled in Elijah's arms. When he saw his mother, he reached out to her. Tears rolled down her cheeks as she said, "Now I know that you are a man of God. And I know that the word of the Lord in your mouth is the truth." In that very instant, Melqart accepted the God of Israel as the only true God.

ENCOUNTER WITH THE PALACE GOVERNOR

Three and a half years had passed and were now gone. The entire region was dusty, to the point of being almost unbearably too miserable for habitation. Very early one morning Elijah was awakened just before the first streaks of the morning light and before the city began to stir. During these two years he had been residing in Zarephath God had been silent. But this morning the quiet voice of God spoke to Elijah, "get up and go for a walk. I need to talk with you." He donned his sandals and descended the staircase which ran alongside the outer wall of the house; so it was easy to leave without awakening either Melqart or Yada.

The morning was cool and pleasant as he walked along the shoreline of the Mediterranean Sea. He stared across the cooling waters while waiting for the voice of God. Finding a place to seat himself he reflected on his call and all the adventures since confronting King Ahab. He was in no hurry to leave this quiet peaceful spot. This seaside piece of land was pleasant and peaceful, an oasis before the noise and clammer of the day. So, Elijah waited, at peace with his surroundings. Into the stillness of the morning, and the quieting of his mind he heard that still small voice, "Elijah. It's time. Go present yourself to Ahab. I am going to send rain on the earth." That was all. It was all that Elijah needed. He had been waiting for three and a half years to hear that brief instruction. It would be far more difficult to tell Melqart and that loving little boy 'good by', this happy little child who had wound his way into this great man's heart.

* * *

Yada's eyes welled up with tears as Elijah squatted down to his level to gently tell him "Good by". It was a painful parting. Melqart and a tearful Yada stood just inside the doorway watching as Elijah slowly walked out of sight. They were a different mother and son than the two fearful, starving people when Elijah entered their lives. Today they were healthy and filled with great hope. The joy that had crept into the house when Elijah had first arrived, would stay with them. Jehovah, had revealed himself through Elijah, and when Elijah had walked away to return to Samaria, the joy and peace remained.

❋ ❋ ❋

The cooling waters of the Mediterranean fell behind as Elijah began the approximately forty-mile trip back to Ahab's palace. It was a dry, dusty, and hot desert: Even more so than his trip toward Zarephath two years earlier. His skin felt as though the moisture was being sucked right out of his body. The sustaining help of God was going to have to keep him going. Elijah looked at the goatskin bag holding his precious supply of water. Would it be enough?

Mile after weary mile of trudging through dust and rocks and heat took their toll. Just when Elijah felt he could not take another exhausting step he looked up and saw a man from a distance. Instantly he knew he had arrived, and this was the one he was supposed to meet. A surge of inner power coursed throughout his body and his pace increased.

✳ ✳ ✳

Obediah was delighted to leave the palace behind for a while. He was a good man, a righteous man. Queen Jezebel was a trial to his very soul with all her idols and the orgies to her wicked, evil Baal as well as all her other disgusting idols. When she had ordered the prophets of the Lord God to be massacred because they disagreed with her idolatrous practices, she swiftly had them purged from the land, and put to a brutal death.

But Obediah was a courageous man who rounded up one hundred of the prophets not yet targeted for annihilation and divided them into two groups, each group hidden in a separate cave. Faithfully he fed them bread and daily saw to it that they had water. This was a dangerous undertaking, but he feared the Lord more than he feared Jezebel.

This mighty man had been entrusted with a great authority; He was the governor of the palace. His responsibilities included the administration as well as the supervision and stewardship, not only over the royal palace, but as well all the other estates the king possessed.

This morning King Ahab had found Obediah and wearily stated, "let's go throughout the land to find any springs of water and any brooks to see if there might be grass for the animals, as the horses and mules must to be kept alive." They agreed that each go in opposite directions to cover more territory.

As they separated, each one going in an opposite direction, Obediah shook his head in frustration. Within the palace walls King Ahab was almost subservient to Jezebel. But outside the palace he seemed to be a somewhat better man, more of a leader, showing a bit more concern in taking more personal responsibilities.

Obediah began his search of the land. Looking up at one point he noticed a man slowly approaching from a distance.

* * *

Obediah was an imposing man who, in his bearing, carried an aura of authority. He now stood silently watching as the approaching man now picked up his pace. As the man drew closer Obediah caught his breath. Could it be? Was it possible? Elijah drew up closer to Obediah who fell on his face terrified in the presence of this powerful man of God. "Is this you, Elijah? Is this really you?"

Elijah reached out his hand to help Obediah to his feet. "Yes, it is I. Now go and tell your master that Elijah is here."

Those words struck terror into Obediah's heart. "How have I sinned that you would say such a thing, that you would actually deliver me into the hands of Ahab to be killed!' Obediah was incredulous. "As the Lord your God lives, there is not a nation nor a kingdom where he has not hunted and searched for you."

Obediah's voice increased in volume as he continued, "he makes these nations and kings to swear by an oath they have not found you. And now, Elijah, you are saying to me I have to find my master and tell him Elijah is here? I know exactly what will happen. As soon as I am out of sight, "poof!", the Lord will pick you up and carry you off to another place that I don't know of. I'll find Ahab and bring him back here and you'll be gone. AND HE WILL CERTAINLY KILL ME!"

Obediah was by now in a state of panic. "What do you have against me? Since I was a child I have feared the Lord. When Jezebel killed God's prophets, I rescued one hundred of them, divided them into two groups of fifty each, hid them into two caves where I took care of them right under Jezebel's nose, every day feeding them bread and water.

"And now, Elijah, you are telling me to find Ahab, bring him here to this very spot, only to find you are gone so that he kills me. What have I done to deserve this?"

Elijah smiled and replied calmly to quiet Obediah's fears. Don't be afraid. I'll be right here when you return. So go in confidence. As the Lord of Host lives, before whom I stand today, I will still be here when you return. I am to present myself before King Ahab today."

In great fear and trembling, Obediah turned away from Elijah to begin the task of locating Ahab. Before too long he saw his master walking slowly trying to find any source of water. When Obediah apprehensively approached his master, Ahab scowled demanding to know why he was here and not out on his search.

"Oh my lord, King Ahab," Obediah stammered out, "I have come to tell you that Elijah is here and is to present himself before you today."

Ahab stared at him, unable to believe his faithful servant. "What did you just say?" He demanded.

Swallowing hard Obediah repeated his message, this time adding Elijah's appearance before him. The king's anger surfaced, demanding that Obediah swear by an oath that it was true. Obediah swore by his statement and the two of them set off together into the direction from which Obediah had come. Two hours later they rounded the crest of a hill and saw a short distance away the form of Elijah.

❋ ❋ ❋

The closer the king drew to his hated enemy, the more his rage surfaced. By the time Ahab was standing directly in front of Elijah his face was contorted in fury. Ahab clenched his teeth together and spat out, "Is this you, oh troubler of Israel?" Ahab's fury knew no bounds. He wanted to murder Elijah right then and there. But God was protecting his servant from this violent king. Elijah never flinched. He was on a divine mission and the real work was about to begin with the message God had sent with him.

Elijah looked unflinchingly into Ahab's face. "I have not troubled Israel. It is you and your father's house who have troubled Israel. Your sins have forsaken the commands and covenants of the God of Israel. You have followed the Baals. Now, you are to gather all of Israel and meet me on the top of Mount Carmel. And there, we will find out once and for all who is the true God."

THE LORD,
HE IS GOD

A hab turned around and headed back to the palace in a huff. But he had no other choice. Elijah was now in charge and he, King Ahab, was required to obey this annoying man who had just ordered he, the king, to invite the entire nation, plus all the prophets of Baal, and all the prophets of Asherah to the top of Mount Carmel. And for what reason? To prove that the God of Israel is the one true God or to prove that the Baals, along with the Asherah were the true gods. But he had to obey. Perhaps the rain clouds would cover the earth and they would finally have rain. A stunned Obediah tried to keep pace with the raging king. For now, anyway, the excursion into the surrounding region had been abandoned. Oh, that they might receive rain on this dry and thirsty land.

Elijah also turned to walk away, only he went back the way he had come. When Obediah turned to look back, he saw only dry, barren land. Elijah had disappeared. Obediah's heart soared and started to sing. The God he worshipped and believed in, the God of Abraham, Isaac, and Jacob, the Creator of the entire world, would prove to be the only true God. With a lighter step he too headed back toward the palace alongside the disbelieving king.

* * *

Elijah headed toward a private area where he could spend quiet time alone with God to prepare his heart and mind for the upcoming contest. He had no doubt that he had delivered the message to the king under the direction of the Lord God. But now he needed more: wisdom, clarity of direction, power. He had to prepare for the upcoming battle. Without divine power he would be helpless before this wicked, adulterous nation, and before the wicked prophets of Baal.

* * *

Elijah was prepared as he headed up Mt. Carmel before the sun had risen into the sky. Only the faint light of dawn provided enough illumination for his journey to the designated spot. Now, one by one the people began to filter up, representatives from every tribe of the Northern Kingdom, and then they arrived by the droves, the prophets of Baal among them. Many of the faces were sullen, others were curious, but here and there scattered among the crowd were faces that showed an understanding of what they were about to be challenged.

Elijah arrived on the mountain divinely imbued with authority and none dared to defy him. He stood before the gathered crowd and when he spoke it was with a God-given confidence with which no one dared argue.

Now as he stood before the people, his presence seemed to fill the entire mountaintop. He wasn't there just to expose the false god, Baal. But his purpose was to bring back a compromising people to the Lord. The evil influences of Ahab and Jezebel had created a nation of people who were lingering between two opinions: to serve both Baal and Jehovah. Elijah was calling them back. They must make a definite decision. Were they going to serve Baal? Were they going to serve Jehovah? They could no longer divide their loyalties. Elijah's voice thundered over the crowd, "If the Lord is God, follow Him. But if Baal is god, follow him." They were speechless. They couldn't respond. They were without true conviction either way.

Elijah continued, "I alone have been left a true prophet of the Lord." He knew there were one hundred prophets secured in two different caves. But he was making a statement that he was the only one openly serving the Lord. He knew he was outnumbered, but also declaring the Lord's power and authority. Therefore, because of that divine anointing he and the Lord God, were a majority.

However, as he stood there looking straight into the crowd, the prophets of Baal's, numbering four hundred and fifty, were smirking and making fun of him. Elijah now addressed them: "Now, may the prophets of Baal take two bulls, and let them choose one for themselves and cut it into pieces. I will cut up the other one. Lay the pieces on the wood. But do not light a fire under the wood. Then you call upon the name of your gods and I will call upon the name of the Lord. The God who answers by fire is the true God.

The people finally responded. "That is well said", was the response.

The prophets of Baal built their altar. They chose their sacrifice. They laid it on the wood. Now they were ready to call out to Baal. "Oh Baal, hear us," were the opening words. Nothing. No response. They began chanting, "Oh Baal, hear us!" Over and over they chanted for his attention. They began dancing. Noon arrived. Nothing! Elijah began to taunt them. "Cry louder! After all, he's a god. Maybe he is meditating. Maybe he's busy. Maybe he's traveling somewhere. Or maybe he's sleeping and needs to be awakened." So the cries increased even more in volume. By now the prophets were cutting themselves with knives and sharp lances; blood running down their bodies and dripping onto the ground.

The frantic cries, and dancing, and cutting of the Baal prophets continued to increase in intensity until the evening sacrifice. But there was no voice. There was no fire. No one answered. No one paid attention.

Then Elijah broke in, inviting the people to come close to him. Each one stepped forward a bit.

It was now three o'clock in the afternoon, the time of the daily evening sacrifice in the temple. "Come in closer to me," he instructed. They stepped even closer to him.

With that, he repaired the broken-down altar and picked up twelve stones, signifying the twelve tribes of the sons of Jacob; reaffirming the unity of God's people when He said to Jacob, "Israel shall be your name."

With the twelve stones Elijah sacredly built the alter in the name of the Lord. Next, he made a trench all around it, large enough to hold a bushel of water. He placed wood on the altar, cut the bull into pieces and laid it on the alter. When that was completed, He chose two young men to fill four water pots from the little Book Kishon. When they had filled them and returned to Elijah, he asked them to pour this water on the sacrifice. "Now, do it again," he instructed. They refiled the waterpots a second time, then a third time, until the trench was running over.

With that, Elijah stepped forward to the altar and simply said, "Lord God of Abraham, Isaac, and Israel, let it be known this day that you are God in Israel, and I am your servant, and that I have done all these things at your word. Hear me, O

Lord, hear me, that this people may know that you are the Lord God, and that You have turned their hearts back to You again" (I Kings 18:36-37 NKJV).

Then the fire fell! It licked up the sacrifice, the wood, the stones, and all the water in the trench. The crowd fell forward with their faces to the ground, loudly declaring, "The Lord, He is God! The Lord, He is God!"

Elijah turned toward the pale, shaken, prophets of Baal who still refused to acknowledge the power of the living God. "Staring at these wicked men he ordered the people standing around, "Seize them, Do not allow one of them to escape. The crowd seized them and Elijah had them taken down to the Brook Kishon, from where the water had come for his sacrifice; and there every one of these false prophets was put to death.

❋ ❋ ❋

The taste of victory was sweet. But the battle had been intense. Elijah was both exhausted and hungry. It had been a long, exhausting fast. Approaching an unhappy and incredulous Ahab, Elijah said to him, "Go eat and drink. I hear the abundance of rain. Ahab left him and went to get something to eat and something to drink.

But Elijah's battle was still not complete. He climbed to the top of Mt. Carmel where he bowed down putting his face between his knees.

THE PROMISED RAIN

Ahab was bitterly disappointed. The day had been long, the prophets who ate at Queen Jezebel's table had all been killed. Elijah had won the contest, and the hearts of the people had been drawn back to Jehovah. Ahab was hungry, thirsty, and dreaded to face his wife. As King Ahab left to physically refresh himself, Elijah turned to climb to the top of the mountain, where he sat, face between his knees. It was time to pray for the promised rains.

✻ ✻ ✻

The battle had been intense. The fire had fallen upon his sacrifice. And it was only at his word that the rains would begin again. His prayer for the rains to stop had been powerful. Now, that same power in prayer would be the beginning for them to restart (James 5:17-18). As with King Ahab, Elijah was also tired and hungry, yet adrenaline was still pumping throughout his system. There was too much still at stake. Unless God sent rain quickly the nation could not survive too much longer. All the sources of water were about to run out. Animals upon which they were dependent were dying off for lack of grass and grains. Crops were no longer producing. The rains were vital for continuation of life.

The god, Baal, with all his abhorrent demands had been defeated. Baal, the god who promised rains and fruitful harvests, had been exposed. Now was the time for God, the absolute creator of heaven and earth; the God who is in all and over all, to come to the aide of the people of Israel: And so he prayed. Elijah finally turned to speak to the young man sitting beside him who sometimes traveled with him. "Go higher and look toward the sea. Come back and tell me what you see."

The young man disappeared for a while and then returned, 'I don't see anything." Elijah continues beseeching God. Again, he sent the young man, and again he returned with the same observation as before, "I don't see anything."

Five more times Elijah fervently beseeched the Lord in prayer, and five more times the young servant climbed the steep incline, scanned the skies over the Mediterranean and then descended the mountain back to where Elijah sat exhausted and drained. Finally, on the seventh descent he was able to excitedly tell Elijah, "I looked toward the sea and there it was, a very small cloud rising out of the sea. I would say it was about the size of a man's hand." Elijah's prayer paid off! He jumped to his feet from his sitting position and began to run. "That's it! God has answered my prayer! Find Ahab! Tell him rain is coming! "

Elijah's adrenaline was now pumping furiously throughout his system. The drought was just about over. Rain was coming. The king had to be told. "Quick! Run! Find Ahab, and tell him to quickly get his chariot ready and leave before the rain stops him." The young man took off running down the mountain to locate Ahab and send him on his way. However, Elijah's adrenalin was still pumping, and he wasn't far behind the racing young man.

The sky rapidly turned black. A wind came up. Off in the distance lightening could be seen and thunder sounded. At first the rain began gently, but rapidly grew in intensity. Heavy raindrops took over and turned the dry ground muddy. But Elijah wasn't about to be deterred. The power of the Lord fell upon Elijah, and he tucked his robe into his belt, overtaking Ahab's chariot with the racing horses anxious to return to their stalls. Elijah picked up speed and never slowed down as he continued to run ahead of Ahab's chariot all the way down the mountain to the gates of Jezreel, about seventeen miles.

Jezebel heard the distant sounds of thunder and smelled the cleanness in the air that signaled rain was about to fall... and glee filled her heart. Could it be? Yes! It was true! Baal, the storm god, had triumphed on Mount Carmel! She began to laugh hysterically. The hated Elijah and his weak Jehovah were defeated, and one way or another they would both soon be out of her hair and out of Israel.

As Jezebel was laughing and congratulating herself a drenched Ahab walked dejectedly through the door. Jezebel felt the first inkling of alarm.

"What's wrong?" She demanded to know. "Why are you so glum? Baal prevailed and now we're rid of that pesky prophet. Look out there! See the falling rain? Baal is alive and well!" And she gave a little seductive dance.

As the longed-for rain filled gullies, streams, and wells with the life-giving liquid the drenched Ahab had arrived back at the palace whining and complaining to Jezebel, as he seated himself, hanging his head low and drooping in defeat. "The prophet Elijah had all the prophets of Baal killed. Baal has been defeated. And the people of Israel have declared that the Lord Jehovah is the true God!" As the king whined to his wife, Jezebel grew coldly rigid.

Ahab continued to talk, still slumped over, still holding his head in his hands. "No Jezebel," he began. "It's terrible. Here's what happened," and he launched into the full accounting ending it with, "And Elijah had all the prophets of Baal killed by the sword, all four hundred and fifty of them, at the Kishon Brook. Not one of them escaped." Jezebel's face turned a chalky white, then a slow red crept up from her neck covering her face. Her face twisted and contorted into a fiery red, violent rage and erupted into a full violence of anger, shrilly demanding a stunned servant standing nearby, "send a letter to that prophet Elijah. Tell him that what he did to my prophets of Baal shall fall upon him by this time tomorrow. He shall die!"

While the life-giving rain continue to fall upon the dried and thirsty land, the cryptic message was delivered to the exhausted, faithful Elijah, "may the gods do to me and even more, if you are not executed by this time tomorrow.

This faithful man of God, this man who had stood fearlessly before an entire nation and declared God to be the only true God: This man who had rid the nation of all the false prophets, was overcome by fear. And he fled for his life.

OVERCOME BY DEPRESSION

Elijah ran as though a thousand demons were chasing him. He took his bewildered servant with him and headed into the direction of Beersheba, the southernmost city in Judah, about one hundred miles. All along the way, as he alternately walked and ran, trying to leave Jezreel as far behind as fast as possible, he berated himself. One word beat an insidious unrelenting drumbeat, over and over, into his head... "Failure! Failure! Failure!" Why had he made such a fool of himself? Why had his mission been such a failure? Why did he feel so abandoned by God? Maybe he had only imagined God had called him to this mission or had called him to only abandon him when the mission had been completed. Nothing made sense.

Elijah didn't realize that all spiritual victories eventually lead to a spiritual attack, that the demons of hell will always try to bring discouragement and despair. They are masters at this. They don't give up their ground without a struggle. And Elijah was especially vulnerable. He was physically and emotionally exhausted. He was in adrenalin depletion. He was physically weak from lack of nourishment, all of which made him a candidate for burnout and ripe for the darkness of depression to set in.

The object of Jezebel's wrath was now out of her reach. But he still felt vulnerable and beyond all reasoning. With every step Elijah took, the nerve wracking, pounding drum beats in his head mercilessly tormented and taunted him. All he wanted to do was to isolate himself and then to die. The question he refused to face was, why had he retreated from an already beaten enemy? But he couldn't reason. He fell headfirst into the pool filled with the lies that he was nothing but a complete miserable failure. The demonic enemies that chased Elijah out of Jezreel and Israel were whispering lies into his mind until depression and despair took him captive. He forgot all the miracles God had heaped upon him for three years. He forgot the vast miracle upon Mount Carmel. He just wanted to die. But God knew where his beloved prophet was, and he never left him; not for a second.

✻ ✻ ✻

Elijah's young servant walked alongside the great man both puzzled and alarmed. He had learned to know Elijah while still in Zarephath. Abirom was still in his teens and had spent many hours talking with Elijah while Elijah talked about Jehovah, the God of Judah and of Israel. He recounted the stories of the world's creation, the Garden of Eden, the fall of man, the stories of Abraham, Isaac, Jacob, the exodus through the Red Sea, and Abirom went from intrigued to acceptance of Jehovah, and turned his back on Baal and all the other gods of idol worship. As he struggled to keep up with the fleeing Elijah, his mind was confused. What happened to all the miracles? Where had all this fear come from that was driving the man, he so admired?

One hundred miles is a long distance on foot. Elijah and Abirom traveled rapidly, taking only a few short breaks and then would continue their puzzling journey. Finally, Beersheba came into view and Elijah turned toward his faithful companion. You stay here while I continue my trip. I'll try to return for you. And with that, Elijah turned into the direction of Mount Horeb, the Mountain of God.

Abirom's heart was pounding as he watched his mentor walk away from him. He didn't know why Elijah had left him just outside of Beersheba. He didn't know that Elijah had left him there for his own safety. He didn't know that Elijah was concerned that it might be possible he was being pursued. He pondered Elijah's parting words, "you stay here. I will try and return to you."

Finally, Abirom turned toward the city. Food, shelter, and sleep were now uppermost in his mind.

✳ ✳ ✳

Elijah was so very weary and now he was alone. He continued his trek further into the wilderness, about another day's journey. Finally, the last physical resource left him, and Elijah found a Broom Tree, which was a Juniper Tree, a flowering shrub that flourishes best in the wilderness areas. It has very thin branches which spread way out offering cooling shade to flocks, herds, and weary, hot travelers such as the prophet, Elijah. These branches are so thin they can be used in binding and make excellent fuel for fires: A wonderful provision given by God for those traveling through the wilderness areas. So, the weary Elijah crawled way under the cooling branches, laid his aching, weary body upon the ground and simply gave up. "Just let me die, Lord; please, just let me die. Take my life. "I am begging you. Take my life. I am no better than my fathers. I have had enough!" And with that he fell into a sound sleep.

Elijah awakened from his deep sleep stupor, completely confused by his surroundings, only to feel a tap on his shoulder. "Elijah, wake up." An angel was standing beside him. As soon as Elijah awakened enough to sit up, the angel disappeared. But the aroma of fresh baked bread sitting on hot coals along with a jug of crisp cold water was enough to trigger all the senses. A sudden onslaught of hunger attacked his stomach, and he ate all the bread, drank the water and sufficiently satisfied Elijah was soon fast asleep again.

Night fell and Elijah slept on. With the early rosy light of morning streaking across the sky the angel once again tapped Elijah. "Wake up, Elijah. Eat and drink because the journey is otherwise too great for you." Elijah got up and once again smelled the warming scent of fresh baked bread. Sitting beside the hot coals containing the bread was another jug of cold water.

Elijah enjoyed his breakfast and slaked his thirst with the refreshing water. Rested, and well fed, he once again resumed his journey. This time, heading toward Mount Horeb, the Mountain of God.

AN ENCOUNTER WITH GOD

As Elijah set out for the next phase of his difficult journey he didn't have any goal or direction in mind. But what he didn't really know or understand was that no longer was he in charge of his own destiny. The unseen presence traveling with him was nudging him, directing him, and pointing him into a very definite area where he was to soon be confronted by the God of all his miracles.

At first, as Elijah set out on his journey from his wilderness campsite, he felt rested and rather enjoyed his new scenery. But as the day and the miles wore on, all the trauma of the past few days returned with lightening force against him, relentlessly driving him onward. Whereas he had delighted in the fields and wildlife and sights when he traveled toward Zarephath and again in the Kerith Ravine, he was now blinded from the surrounding environment. Now his state of mind was anxious and troubled, unable to take in any beauty or delight. Depression and ever increasing fears had taken hold and were blinding him to anything other than his terror and fears. So Elijah plodded along, not really sure of where he was going, or even why.

The angel of the Lord who had fed him, nourishing his body, back under the Broom Tree, was now encompassing him, giving him hour by hour and moment by moment strength for that journey. But Elijah was too blinded and too depressed to even notice. On the miraculous and amazing strength of that nourishment Elijah traveled another forty days and forty nights.

Mt. Sinai, also known as Mt. Horeb, rose before him: The hallowed place where God had given the Ten Commandments to Moses. Mt. Sinai, the Mountain of God, came into view... the mountain where Moses had been given the law. With decreasing strength, he began the upward climb of the 4500 feet of the mountain, until he came upon a cave opening. Not concerned by the possibility that the interior could possibly be inhabited by some wild beast, he stumbled inside and collapsed with fatigue and weakness and there he slept soundly throughout the rest of the day and through the night hours with no disturbance. The protective presence of God's angels watched carefully and lovingly over their beloved Elijah, giving him warmth and comfort.

The penetrating caw of a large bird broke into his consciousness, bringing him to a sleepy wakefulness. Yawning, he sat up, and after getting his bearings he noticed through the cave opening that the sun had traveled high into the sky. "Oh", he thought, "I must have slept throughout all of yesterday and well into the next day!"

But, now what? Elijah had fled from Israel over the very real threat hanging over his life. If he left the cave that threat was possibly still out there. Depressed, dejected, and feeling utterly defeated, he had no idea where he could go nor what he could do. He sat up with his back against the wall of the cave, knees bent and with his arms wrapped around his legs, burying his face between his knees. As far as he was concerned, he had no hope. Elijah faced the terrible reality that his life was pretty much over, that he was a failure, no use to God, to himself, or to anybody else.

* * *

Elijah sat alone and dejected, face between his knees having no idea where or go or what to do now that he had ended up here in this damp, miserable cave, this place of retreat, If he left this cave he was as good as dead. But if he stayed here, he was also as good as dead. He was hungry. He was thirsty, and he felt weak, and he couldn't imagine that anything would automatically appear before him. He let out a long, frustrated groan. He was too hungry and thirsty and too miserable to even think straight. Then suddenly, a voice filled the room. It was a voice he had heard time and time again. "Elijah, what are you doing here?" Elijah's face disappeared even further into his knees. The voice sounded fearsome to his addled mind. He had run as far as he could run from a wicked king and from an even more wicked Jezebel, from a nation, and even from God Himself. And now he had been found. He let out another loud groan of despair. But he could not escape that voice. "What are you doing here, Elijah?"

Elijah not only felt hungry, thirsty, dejected and in despair, but also a bit rebellious as well as very frustrated and petulant. So, he replied, "I have been very zealous for the Lord God of hosts; for the children of Israel have forsaken Your covenant, torn down Your altars, and killed Your prophets with the sword. I alone am left; and they seek to take my life." There, that should explain it. But God was not about to let it go.

"Go out and stand on the mountain before the Lord." With that a tremendous strong wind came up, shaking the mountain. It tore into the mountain breaking up rocks into pieces. But the Lord wasn't in the wind. Following the wind an earthquake shook the mountain, but neither was the Lord in the earthquake. Following the earthquake, a huge fire broke out upon the mountain, but again, the Lord was not in the fire. Then, a discernible; but very small, gentle voice spoke into the cave where Elijah still sat huddled against the wall. Elijah now stood to his feet wrapping his face into his mantle and went out to stand in the entrance of the cave. The voice spoke once again, "What are you doing here, Elijah?"

Still feeling petulant, although not quite as defensive as he had felt earlier, Elijah once again replied. "I have been very zealous for the Lord God of hosts; because the children of Israel have forsaken Your covenant, torn down Your altars, and killed Your prophets with the sword. I alone am left; and they seek to take my life."

The wind, the earthquake, the fire were mighty demonstrations of God's power over nature. And Elijah had used those demonstrations on Mt. Carmel: The fire, the wind, and the rainstorm. He was acquainted with that power. But when he heard the still, small voice, he responded, going out to meet the God who had spoken to him and ministered mighty miracles through His servant.

Then God did what only a loving Heavenly Father could do. He neither scolded nor accused his servant. Instead, He ministered to him. He had his angel prepare some food and drink. He comforted His servant. And He set him free of his fears and depression. After Elijah was sufficiently refreshed, then God spoke again.

"I am not finished with your ministry. I want you to return the way you came. Return to Beersheba. Abirom is still there waiting for you. Then head into the Wilderness of Damascus. When you arrive at the Wilderness of Damascus find Hazel and anoint him to be king over Syria. Then find Jehu, the son of Nimshi, and anoint him to be king over Israel. Next, I want you to find Elisha, the son of Shaphat. You are to anoint him as the prophet in your place. And Elijah, you are not the only one left. I have reserved seven thousand who live in Israel who have not bowed to Baal, nor have kissed him. You have never been alone.

ELISHA'S CALLING

Elisha sleepily sat up on the edge of his cot, tucking his feet under him. Was it really time to get up? Surely, he must have just crawled into bed; but sadly yes, the sky was streaked with the first rays of the morning sun. With a deep sigh of resignation Elisha crawled off his cot and slipped into his clothes. That endless field was not going to plow itself. It was the start of a new day. But what he did not know, was that God had a surprise in store for him... that this day was about to turn his life upside down.

Elisha went outdoors to locate his team of oxen. Eleven other men were collecting their teams of two each and heading into the fields belonging to Elisha's family. Unlike most families, Elisha came from a wealthy family that owned twelve teams of oxen to plow their large fields. Elisha hooked up his team and turned toward the field for which he was responsible.

* * *

The mighty prophet, Elijah had been a very busy man. After his desperate flight to the cave at Mt. Horeb, God had comforted him, fed him, and picked him back up, dusted him off; assuring him that the next assignments would be successful. Renewed in his spirit, Elijah left the cave returning to duty. First, he retrieved his relieved servant, Abirom from the city of Beersheba. Abirom would remain with Elijah until they entered back into Samaria. From Beersheba the two men headed into Syria where Elijah anointed Hazel, who was a servant to King Ben-hadad to be king over that Gentile nation. Next, Elijah located Jehu, who was captain of King Ahab's army to replace Ahab. It was there that Elijah bid Abirom good-by. And now he was headed 150 miles from Sinai to Abel Meholah, located in the Jordan Valley, where he would find Elisha plowing his field.

God had a plan. Israel had turned away from God and it seemed as though the nation as a whole, had turned to depravity and unspeakable wickedness. But while Elijah sat immersed in self-pity in the Mt. Horeb cave feeling as though all his efforts had been in vain, God had revealed to him that there was still a remnant of 7,000 within the nation of Israel. Among the 7,000 was a young man named Elisha who was presently busy plowing his family's field.

Elijah's wild dash to Mt. Horeb had been driven by fear, deep pain, and grief. He felt all his efforts had failed. He grieved that the present generation was too far gone. He grieved that there was no hope for the future of Israel. But unknowing to him, God was raising up a new generation, and Elijah's job was to anoint the two kings and a prophet who would help to equip this new generation. And a very large part of Elijah's job would be to mentor and help equip this young new prophet.

* * *

Hour after weary hour the oxen plodded on while Elisha plodded behind them, with the overhead sun ruthlessly baking him. "Now I know how a roasting calf feels" he miserably mumbled to himself. While the sun was still high in the sky, he called a halt to his laboring oxen and stood still to rest a moment and brush perspiration out of his eyes as well as to take a long drink from his goatskin bag. A glance into the sky told him there were several more hours to go before he could trudge home for his evening meal. Sighing, he picked up the reigns instructing the laboring oxen to continue on again. But wait! Someone, a man, was crossing the field heading straight toward Elisha. Once again Elisha told the oxen to stop while he watched this dusty man who was obviously coming straight toward him. As the man got closer Elisha caught and held his breath. Was it? Could it really be? Was the great prophet, Elijah really here in his field heading straight into his direction?

Elisha held his breath as Elijah drew closer. And then he was there, standing right in front of him, not saying a word while holding his mantle (or outer garment) in his hands. Still not saying a word Elijah threw his garment over the head of the stunned young man who instantly knew what had happened. He, Elisha, had just been commissioned to become Elijah's servant and then to become his successor. It was a high honor and a solemn responsibility.

Elisha stood for a moment in stunned silence. In that moment while he held his breath trying to take it all in, and in that same moment realizing the enormity of his entire life change: Never for a second did he hesitate to enter this God given task and Divine call of this great adventure ahead of him. He, and his family, were a part of this remnant God had preserved for himself. Elisha felt humbled and grateful to now serve alongside of this man he so deeply admired.

When he could finally speak, Elisha ran after Elijah who had turned to walk away. "Wait," he called. "I need to kiss my parents good-by."

"Go ahead. I'm not stopping you." Elijah replied.

Elisha hurried home to tell his parents what had just occurred. Then he took his wooden farm implements, burned them and slaughtered his two oxen roasting them in the fire set from the wooden farm implements. When the meat was done, he fed his family, Elijah, and himself, as well as other people around them. Now that he had burned all his bridges behind him, a humbled Elisha then turned to Elijah quietly stating, "I'm ready to follow you and to serve you

IN THE SHADOW OF ELIJAH

W alking away from his family home was bitter-sweet. Elisha felt honored to be walking alongside this great man who had made such an enormous impact upon his life. On the other hand, he felt torn to be leaving behind all that was familiar and dear to his heart. Then there was the unknown: What would this new life be like? What was really to be expected of him? All he knew was farming. But like Elijah, Elisha possessed a great sorrow and burden for his nation of Israel. This was indeed an enormous calling God was placing upon his life... to intercede and fight for a sinful, broken people and a nation that had lost its way.

The two men walked silently side by side for a while until finally Elisha broke the silence. "I feel honored to be chosen by you to be your servant. But it's all a bit overwhelming. You will need to teach me what I need to know." He stopped talking, embarrassed to show his ignorance.

Elijah didn't say anything for a while then finally spoke. "No, my son, I didn't choose you. God chose you. He is the one who sent me to find you. He told me you would be plowing in the field. Your job is to go where I go. You are to learn from me; because some day you too will become a prophet to help bring our people, Israel, back to Himself.

Elijah's words sent a thunderbolt sensation throughout Elisha's system. The enormity of the responsibility before him was overwhelming. "Can I really do this?" He whispered to himself. "Am I really capable of doing this?"

He didn't know his anxious whispered response had reached the ears of great prophet. "Yes, my son," Elijah replied. "When God calls, he provides everything needed for the task." Elisha stifled an inner groan. The overwhelming feeling was still rattling around inside of him.

After what seemed like a very long trek

through the countryside, Elijah finally found a large rock and sat down to rest. Feeling exhausted from the day, the young protege promptly sat on the ground, folding his legs in front of him, enormously grateful to finally be able to rest. This had been a bewildering day and he was trying his best to take it all in.

Elisha peered at the sky and noticed the sun hanging low in the west. The steep encampments bordering the Jordan Valley were by now glowing with the purple rays of the setting sun. Wondering about the nighttime hours Elisha finally asked the question weighing on his mind, "Uh, where will we sleep tonight?"

A hint of an amused smile played across Elijah's features. "Why, we'll camp out right here tonight and continue our journey tomorrow."

Elisha looked around the hard ground underneath and around him, finally answering in a small voice, "Um, ok", as visions of his comfortable bed and walled in house played across his mind. This was rapidly becoming an exercise in the development of a toughened lifestyle. Elijah found a slight indention on the ground, tucked his mantle into a pillow and allowed himself a chuckle.

* * *

Elijah wasted no time drifting off to sleep, loud snores quickly punctuating the stillness of the night. But Elisha could not sleep. His brain twisted and turned into a tangle of images, thoughts, sounds, voices... the voices of his parents telling their son a brave "good-by". They were proud of him, proud that God had called him into such a noble calling; but at the same time feeling the pain of his departure. Scenes of the countryside floated in and out of his mind, Elijah walking silently beside him, along with his voice assuring him that God would provide everything Elisha would need when the time came that he would become the successor. That's what scared him the most: becoming the successor of this great and powerful Elijah! When would it happen? How would it happen? Would he even begin to be prepared for such a time as this? Elisha stretched out on the uncomfortable ground feeling he could never fall asleep. His eyes roamed across the sky studying the tapestry of stars above him. The light of a full moon lit up the surrounding land with a soft glow. Gradually a calmness settled over the troubled soul of Elisha, and he drifted off into an untroubled sleep. His last conscience thought was, "Whatever it takes, I will answer this calling." All the while, the ever-watchful eye of a loving God surrounded the two who were resting peacefully in the safety of His great outdoors.

IN THE SCHOOL OF EXPERIENCE

King Ahab, king over Israel, was upset. He was so upset that he slunk drooping into the palace, went straight into his bed chamber, laid down and pouted. Nobody could please him and he could not be tempted to feel better, no matter what anyone did to try and lift his spirits. He only turned his back to everyone, whining, complaining, and snapping at his unfortunate servants, his personal servant sighed, rolling his eyes with frustration. Whenever the king was sullen and pouted, he could be very difficult to please.

Finally, Queen Jezebel approached. "What's wrong?" She asked. "Why are you lying here in this bed so unhappy?"

Sounding like a petulant child he whined, 'Because Naboth won't sell me his vineyard. I want it for a vegetable garden. But he says it's his family's inheritance and he will not give it to me. His excuse was that God gave it to his family as an inheritance. I even told him I would pay well for it, or even give him a better vineyard in its' place. But, no, he won't even listen to me. It's not fair. I'm the king. He should give it to me." His voice trailed off in a sob of self-pity.

Jezebel knew instantly what needed to be done. "Leave it to me. You're the king over all Israel. Get out of bed, get something to eat and cheer up. I will get you the vineyard." And with that assurance King Ahab rolled out of bed, ordered some food knowing the vineyard was as good as his. Jezebel always knew what to do.

* * *

The wonderful odor of frying fish awakened a sleepy Elisha. He sat up, scanning his surroundings as memory slowly returned to his groggy brain. He glanced into the direction of Elijah who looked over at him and smiled. "Would you like some breakfast? Elisha enthusiastically nodded his head. He could swear his stomach was rubbing painfully against his backbone. But wait! Where had Elijah found fish to fry?

Elijah laughed and responded, "If you look over that embankment you will notice the Jordan River. They've got some good fish swimming around just waiting to be caught. Elisha grinned sheepishly. He had temporarily forgotten where they had spent the night.

A satisfying breakfast of freshly fried fish, refreshing themselves in the cold river, and the two were ready to resume their journey.

As they were setting out Elisha timidly inquired, "My Lord, where are we going?"

Elijah replied, "we are going into Samaria to meet Ahab, the king. He is in the vineyard of Naboth. King Ahab has had Naboth put to death and stolen his vineyard. God has instructed me to pronounce a judgement against him for the murder of Naboth so he could steal the vineyard." Elisha swallowed hard. Would he be called upon to make such declarations after assuming the role of a prophet?

❊ ❊ ❊

Jezebel wasted no time. How dare anyone, especially a farmer like Naboth, deny the king what the king wanted! She promptly sent a letter, in Ahab's name, sealed it with his seal, and sent a messenger to the elders of the city of Jezreel which was adjacent to Naboth's vineyard. This letter instructed them to proclaim a fast and to place Naboth in a prominent place and then to send in two reprobates to sit in front of him. They were to declare they heard him blaspheming. With that the elders were to drag him out of the city, along with his two sons, where they were all three to be stoned to death.

Jezebel was elated at her creativity. According to the law, a public criminal's property could be seized and revert to the king. 'Ingenious', Jezebel thought as she congratulated herself. Equally as elated as Jezebel for her act of genius, Ahab stopped his pouting and hurried from the palace to claim the coveted property. But neither Jezebel nor Ahab had any idea that God's judgement was about to fall upon each of them because of all their great wickedness.

* * *

When Elijah had awakened that first morning after Elisha had joined him, he awoke to the voice of God giving directions for his next assignment. The message was clear. "Get up and go down to meet Ahab. You will find him in Naboth's vineyard. This is what you shall say, 'Thus says the Lord. Have you murdered and taken possession? In the place where dogs licked the blood of Naboth, dogs shall lick your blood.'" A tough message to deliver to anyone, even a wicked king.

As they neared the palace Elisha asked rather uneasily, "Where do we go when we arrive?"

Elijah simply responded, "straight to the vineyard of Naboth. That's where we will find the king."

* * *

As Elijah and Elisha were entering the area of Jezreel, Ahab could be found strutting up and down all the luscious rows of grapes, proudly admiring his new acquisition. He stopped to admire an imposing cluster of grapes when an uncomfortable shadow fell over him. Looking up, all he could blurt out was a terrified, "Have you found me my enemy?" If he had been open to truth, Ahab would have been forced to recognize that it was he who was his own worst enemy.

Without an opening statement or greeting Elijah looked straight into his eyes and replied, "Yes, I have found you. And your sins have found you. The Lord has sent me to you to deliver this message: 'Because you have sold yourself to do evil in the sight of the Lord, I will bring calamity upon you. I will take away your posterity and remove every male from your household because of the way you have provoked me. You have murdered Naboth and have taken possession of what was rightfully his. You have sold yourself too evil. Therefore, in the place where dogs licked the blood of Naboth, dogs shall lick your blood and Jezebel will be eaten by dogs by the wall of Jezreel."

Ahab's body began an uncontrollable tremble. He tore his clothes and put on sackcloth (a very course, rough fabric made of flax or hemp). He fasted and went around in mourning and repentance.

Then God spoke to Elijah. "Because Ahab has humbled himself and repented, I shall not bring this calamity upon him and upon his house during his lifetime, but during the days of his son."

* * *

Three years passed from the last time Syria and Israel had been in battle. But Ahab became restless. The Syrian king, Ben-hadad had taken some cities during the last conflict and had made an agreement with Ahab they would be returned to Israel. But it hadn't yet taken place. Therefore, Ahab asked Jehoshaphat, King of Judea to join him in this battle to take back these cities. God wasn't pleased that Jehoshaphat agreed to come alongside of Ahab in this conflict; however, Jehoshaphat was a righteous king and God allowed it to happen. It was in this battle that Ahab suffered a mortal wound, As Elijah had predicted, His blood ran onto the floor of the chariot. That evening someone washed the chariot at a pool in Samaria and the dogs licked up his blood.

* * *

Ahab's body was buried in Samaria and his son Ahaziah, was crowned to ascend the throne of Israel where he reigned for two years. Ahaziah was every bit as evil as his father, Ahab and his mother,

Jezebel. Like his parents he worshipped Baal and provoked the Lord God of Israel to anger.

CHARIOT AND HORSES OF FIRE

As Elijah had prophesied, God had finally been so thoroughly provoked by all the evil practices of the Israelite kings, that Omni's dynasty was fast coming to an end. Therefore, the new king, Ahaziah took a nasty tumble, falling through a lattice in an upper room, ending up in bed where he suffered greatly from all his wounds. But In spite of the warnings of godly prophets, as well as Elijah's stern rebukes to his father, Ahab; Ahaziah refused to pay any attention to any of it. Instead, he sent messengers to Ekron, located forty miles from his palace to inquire of that Baal if he was going to recover from these severe injuries.

But God knew what was simmering in the heart of this wicked king and he sent an angel to inform Elijah the plans of King Ahaziah, who was planning to inquire of their Baal whether he would live. Surely, no one would know of his secret inquiry, he thought. But God knew. Therefore, the angel of God revealed the entire plan to Elijah and told him exactly where to meet these messengers. To their complete surprise he approached asking, "Is it because there is no God in Israel that you are going to inquire of Baal, the god of Ekron? Go back to King Ahaziah and tell him that he shall surely die."

Understandably, the messengers were startled. How had this strange man known where they were going and why? But they responded to his instructions, turned around and returned to the bedchamber of their king. When they slowly approached him, he demanded rather crossly, "Why have you come back?"

The leader of the messengers replied, "We hadn't gone very far when a strange man approached us and told us to return to the king. This is what he said, 'The Lord says, Is it because there is no God in Israel that you send to inquire of Baal, the god of Ekron? Therefore, Ahaziah shall not live. He shall surely die'."

Ahaziah's face twisted in fury. "Who was this man! What did he look like!"

The messengers almost tumbled over each other as they nervously attempted to reply. "He was a hairy man, dressed in a camel skin. And he was wearing a leather belt around his waist."

Ahaziah's face hardened as he bit out, "It is Elijah the Tishbite and he will not get away with this!"

The next morning the king sent a captain along with fifty men to meet Elijah who was sitting calmly on the top of a hill. The captain ordered Elijah to go with him. But Elijah refused. He knew the king had ordered him to be killed. Elijah replied, "If I am a man of God, as you have just mentioned, then He will send fire from heaven to consume you and your men." Instantly fire hit the captain and killed him as well as all fifty men.

The enraged Ahaziah was not deterred. He ordered another uneasy captain of fifty men to replace the first captain and his destroyed men. They were also told to bring Elijah in. Again, he was found on the top of the hill and again fire fell from heaven and destroyed all of them. Ahaziah was beside himself with frustration. So, he sent out yet another captain with fifty men under him. But this time it was different. This young captain approached Elijah with respect. He fell on his knees before Elijah, beseeching him to please allow him to live. "Man of God, please allow my life and the lives of these men under me to live. May my life and the lives of these men be precious in your sight." Then the angel of the Lord spoke to Elijah, giving him permission to go with this captain, and to present himself before the king.

When Elijah walked through the door of the king's bedchamber, he boldly approached the suffering king and wasted no time to give him this message, "Because you sent messengers to inquire of Baal in Ekron whether you would live, you shall die. Is it because there is no God in Israel of whom to inquire as to whether you will live? Because you sought Baal for answers, you shall die. And he did die. That very night his soul was required of him.

* * *

Elijah's days were fast ending. He and Elisha had spent almost ten years together. Elisha had enjoyed the privilege of being taught and mentored by Elijah. Those had been precious days and years. Now, both Elisha and Elijah were aware they were on their final journey together. After confronting Ahaziah the two men traveled to the area of Gilgal. Before God took him, Elijah needed to visit three schools of prophets and minister to them. These three schools of prophets were dedicated men who were called of God to study the scriptures and teach the people. It was their responsibility to call the people back to the obedience of his covenant.

Elijah frequently visited these schools, ministering to these men, teaching them in the scriptures how to instruct the people. As Elijah was leaving the school in Gilgal, he asked Elisha to remain as the Lord was sending him about fifteen miles on to Bethel to the next school. But Elisha refused. "No. I am not leaving you." Elijah nodded his head and they continued from Gilgal to Bethel.

When they arrived in Bethel, some of the prophets approached Elisha asking, "Did you know the Lord is taking your master from you today?"

Elisha replied, "Yes, I know that. Don't say anything more about it." It was too painful to talk about.

There, in Bethel, Elijah once again told

Elisha, "Please stay here. For the Lord has now sent me another fifteen miles on to Jericho."

But Elisha cried out in anguish, "No, I must go with you. As surely as the Lord lives, and as surely as you live, I cannot leave you!" So together they continue their journey toward Jericho.

When they arrived in Jericho this group of prophets approached Elisha stating, "did you know the Lord is taking your master away from you today?"

Elisha responded in pain at the revelation, "Yes, I know this. But please, keep quiet about it."

Once again Elijah spoke to his faithful servant, "Elisha, this time stay here. The Lord has spoken to me again and instructed me to go on to the Jordan."

But Elisha cried out, "No. I must go with you! I cannot leave you!" And again, they set out, this time about five miles toward the Jordan River. The two men were now continuing the final leg of their journey together. Elijah's final moments of teaching and training were now over. And Elisha was asking his final questions. As they approached the river, Elijah asked Elisha an important question before he was taken away from him. "What would you like me to give you?"

These treasured moments of Elijah's legacy were Elisha's gift of ministry. Now, Elijah was leaving behind a prepared servant to carry on his ministry. And Elisha was prepared with his answer, "Please give me a double portion of your spirit."

This response in his moment of intense grief was the desire of a double measure of Elijah's faithfulness, courage, and obedience. He wanted to bring the ministry that Elijah had begun to a completeness which would require a huge measure of God's help.

The Jordan River was before them. A group of about fifty prophet's stood in the distance as the two men approached the waters of the river. They saw Elijah take off his mantle, roll it up, and the waters parted. The two crossed over on dry land. When they reached the other side, the waters came back together again.

The two had walked only a short distance when it happened! Suddenly a chariot of fire appeared with horses of fire, separating the two of them. Elijah was caught up into a whirlwind and then shot up into the heavens. Elisha cried out in anguish, "My father! My father! the chariot of Israel and its horsemen;" meaning this man, this powerful man of God, had been equivalent to an entire army in his obedience and courage for God and the nation of Israel.

As suddenly as the chariot and the horses had appeared, they were gone again. Elisha kept gazing up for a few moments. Then he saw it: Elijah's mantle. He bent over, picked it up and grief-stricken turned to retrace their steps. He approached the river. As Elijah had done, Elisha rolled up the mantle and struck the waters. The waters parted and Elisha crossed over on dry ground.

A DOUBLE PORTION

The men standing a distance from the Jordan saw only Elisha slowly return. He approached the river. They watched silently as he stood on the bank, struck the water with Elijah's mantle and then cried out, "Where is the Lord God of Elijah?" With his cry the waters parted, giving him a dry path between the waters.

When Elisha crossed to the opposite bank the prophets hurried to meet him, quickly recognizing that the spirit of Elijah now rested on him, and they bowed before him. The men then asked would you permit us to search for Elijah? Perhaps the Spirit of God has left him on a mountain or in a valley somewhere? At first, he refused because he knew Elijah had been taken into heaven. But they persisted until he finally gave permission. After three days the men returned to Jericho empty-handed and he couldn't resist saying, "I told you you would not find him."

Elisha was eager to begin his ministry but before he could leave Jericho, he was approached by several men of the city who pointed out what a pleasant city Jericho was except, they said, "the water is terrible. Things won't grow. The ground is barren: could you do something about it?"

After a few moments of contemplation he said, "bring me a new bowl with salt in it. He took the bowl containing the salt, then located the source of the water and declared, "The Lord says, 'I have healed the water; from it there shall be no more death or barrenness.'" Instantly, the water became pure and sweet.

Elisha left Jericho headed toward Samaria by way of Bethel. Before he could enter the city some wayward teens saw him coming and thought they would have some fun at his expense. "Hey you baldheaded man. Where are you going? Think you'll be welcomed in Bethel?" They continued taunting, laughing, and mocking him.

Finally, Elisha had enough of their disrespect, so he turned around and pronounced a curse upon them. The mob of teens burst into a mocking laugh until they saw two female bears bounding their way out of the woods. The bears leaped on them, mauling forty-two teenagers. Elisha now turned toward Samaria.

* * *

These past few days had been physically and emotionally draining. As he headed into the direction of Mt. Carmel and Samaria, Elisha now had time and quiet to think, pray, and contemplate about what all had happened as well as to come to terms with the ministry he was continuing from Elijah's teaching and mentoring.

Elisha reflected over the vast expanse of Elijah's ministry. He considered the power of the pyrotechnics that occurred on Mt. Carmel. Mere man could never accomplish what Elijah had done throughout his lifetime: Mt. Carmel, praying for no rain; then praying for it to rain; being fed by ravens; the mysterious divine refilling of oil and flour during the famine when Elijah had been cared for by a poor widow lady; the raising of her son when he had died. How did Elijah know what to do in each case? What was his secret?

Then Elisha recalled: How had he known what to do when he returned to the Jordan River after seeing Elijah taken from him? How did he know the answer for the bitter water to be healed in Jericho? The answer was prayer!

Being with Elijah had been a rich experience. He knew Elijah was just a man. Elijah had experienced doubts and fears and even depression while running from Jezebel. He had react as a man. He experienced disappointments. He had human frailties and faults. The secret, Elisha admitted, was in his prayer life. Elijah would wait upon God in prayer, listen for the answer, and act upon it., always seeking for God to be glorified. Elijah didn't doubt the answers when he heard them. He was well acquainted with God's voice and would act upon God's direction, exactly as God had given instruction: Why? Because he trusted God's leadership. It wasn't Elijah who performed the miracles. It was God using a human man who was courageous enough to allow Him to work in and through his humanness. Now God had anointed a very human Elisha to continue this vital ministry.

Elisha had to stop and sit on a rock with this astounding revelation. He had known the reality of Elijah's power and prayer life. But now that he no longer had Elijah to take the lead, he must continue the ministry with the same deep intercessory prayers of Elijah. Elisha had never really thought it completely through until this moment. Like a thunderbolt out of the sky; he realized that he too, had only one recourse if he was to be effective in this powerful ministry to which he had been called. Like Elijah, he too must be a faithful prayer intercessor and courageously respond to God's voice, just as Elijah had courageously responded to the divine directions he had been given.

Elisha closed his eyes and wept. The call was awesome, enormous, greater than he could ever fulfill in his humanness. But, God was even more awesome, enormous, and infinitely greater than he, Elisha could ever be. With that assurance, Elisha stood to his feet to continue his journey.

THRUST INTO MINISTRY

Elisha didn't have long to wait before he was thrust headfirst into a major conflict. It had to do with three kings who were heading rather blindly into a sticky war situation. And Elisha had to set them straight. The kings of Israel, Judah, and Edom were on their way to make war against Moab. Moab was, basically, keeping Israel hostage over a tribute the king of Moab refused to pay when a young King Jehoram took over the throne of Israel. The land of Moab was ideal for the raising of sheep. And Moab rebelled over the 100,000 lambs and 100,000 rams' wool tribute they were required to pay each year to Israel. So, the youthful King Jehoram summoned the kings of Judah and Edom to join him into making war on Moab over the unpaid tributes.

They had set out on a rather good plan to surprise the Moabites. Jehoram's army left Samaria, picked up Judah's, probably in Jerusalem, then the two armies headed south toward Edom, where Edom's army joined the other two. They were taking a roundabout route toward the more vulnerable southern Moab border. It was a good plan, except after seven days of marching they ran out of water and there was none for neither man nor beast. It evolved into a desperate situation. Finally, Judah's King Jehoshaphat asked a simple question, "Is there not a man of God who can give us some wise advice?"

The other two kings looked at one another and shrugged. Neither of them had a clue. But one of Jehoram's officers overheard and volunteered, "Yes, there is. The prophet, Elisha is right here. He joined the troops a while back."

Why Elisha joined the troops was considered a mystery. Why would he do that? But with God it was not a mystery. He knew the three armies were entering into a desperate situation so he whispered to his prophet to quietly join the armies because unless they sought Him, they could weaken and die in the dry desert. And now King Jehoshaphat was alerted to seek the Lord through one of God's faithful prophets. And Elisha was already prepared.

With all the men chattering, desperate for relief, the din was extremely distracting. And no matter how close Elisha was with God, he could not hear himself think nor could he shut out all the noise to concentrate.

"I need a musician," he ordered. "Someone finds a musician and bring him to me." Everyone looked at everyone else. This was a strange request. When did a prophet need a musician brought to him? A scurrying about located a young harpist in their midst. He was brought to Elisha. As the sweet notes filled the air, the men quieted, and Elisha could focus and a blessed quietness entered into his heart and mind. Then he could hear the Lord speak into his heart.

The men were to spread out and dig ditches into the dry valley. The men hastened to obey. That night it rained in the mountains. There was no wind, nor was there any storm: Just a nice cooling rain which ran down the sides of the mountains filling the ditches with refreshing water. There was more than enough for both man and beast.

* * *

The nation of Moab had received the alarming news that Israel, Judah, and Edom were on the way to declare war against them. So, the king of Moab, Mesha, quickly gathered all his army together and went out to meet the three kings. The next morning, they arrived at the dry valley only to see it filled with flooded water. But it didn't look like actual water. It was blood red. King Mesha was filled with glee.: Blood! It was blood... he thought. It was the reflection of the sun on the pools of flooded water giving the illusion of blood. King Mesha lost no time sending his soldiers into the camps of the three kings. He thought the three armies had turned on each other. In sending his soldiers into the camps he felt confident of their safety and the wealth they would collect.

But the Moabites had been under a delusion. They advanced joyfully, noisily, and eagerly into the midst of a slaughter... their own slaughter. The Moabite army turned tail and fled, pursued by the three armies. Then the armies of Israel, Judah, and Edom entered the land of Moab, where they stopped up the water with stones, destroyed their fortified cities, and denuded the land, just as Elisha had instructed. It was a guarantee that the people of Moab would be unable to regroup and fight back.

* * *

The three nations were successful. They destroyed the cities of Moab. Each man threw a stone on every piece of good land. They stopped up every spring and well of good water. They destroyed every good tree. It was a perfect defeat. King Mesha was completely devastated. He took seven hundred sword welding men and tried to break through to the King of Edom, but the battle was too fierce. In his bitterness of spirit King Mesha took his son, his eldest son, the crown prince, to the top of the wall and there offered him to the god Chemosh, the Moabite deity, as a burnt sacrifice.

This so enraged and disgusted both the Moabites and the three kings at this deplorable act, that they ceased fighting and returned to their own lands. It was a victory, but at a terrible price.

ELISHA MINISTERS GRACE

E lisha settled into his ministry with great grace, putting into practice his mentor's secret of prayer. As his ministry took form Elisha was developing a heart of great compassion and wisdom. But he was also as fearless and as courageous as Elijah had been when it came down to declaring truth when men, even kings resisted it.

Elisha had inherited Elijah's responsible position to be a itinerate teacher for the different schools of prophets which were in several different areas. One day a woman approached him as he was instructing a class of these prophets. She was care warn and obviously under great stress. A desperation of words poured out of her as she sobbed before him: "My husband, Obadiah is dead. He hid one hundred prophets when Jezebel set out to kill those who refused to bow down and worship Baal. You knew him. You know how he loved and feared the Lord. He borrowed money in order to preserve these one hundred prophets and I cannot pay the creditors. They are coming to carry my two sons and me away to be slaves. I am desperate. I don't know what to do!"

Elisha looked upon this agonizing woman with deep compassion. He knew this man's reputation as a very courageous and godly man. Now with his death his widow would certainly have a difficult time making ends meet. Thoughtfully, Elisha asked her, "what do you have in your home?"

She responded with, "only a small amount of oil."

"Here's what you do," he told her. "Have your sons go around to your neighbors and borrow every empty jar they can locate. Then take the jars and your sons inside, close your door and pour your oil into each jar, filling it to the top. Next, take those full jars of oil, sell the oil, and pay your creditors. There will be enough left over for you and your sons to live on."

Greatly encouraged and with hope seeping into her heart, this widow of the courageous man, Obediah, sent her boys out into the community to collect all the empty vessels they could locate. They took them into the house and shut the door just as Elisha had instructed. She then filled each jar with an amazing never-ending oil. The three then went out, sold all of the oil, and hastened to pay the creditors. Obadiah's widow wept with relief as her tormenting fears vanished. The two boys could hardly take in the joyful release of their deepest fears. That night, mother, and sons rejoiced and were able to sleep soundly because of God's deliverance through the compassion and wisdom of this man of God. Now this family were privileged to experience a great miracle of grace., just as one hundred men of God had experienced a miracle of Grace through the courage of their father and husband, the man Obediah.

* * *

One of the towns Elisha frequently visited was

Shunem. Shunem lay approximately three miles north of Jezreel, twenty miles northwest from Elisha's hometown, and about twenty five miles or so beyond Shunem was Mt. Carmel.

On one particularly hot day Elisha and his servant, Gehazi were walking through Shunem when a lady, approached the two men and invited them to her home to eat a meal with her and her household. This woman had considerable wealth and enjoyed a great standing as well as quite influential in her community. Elisha and Gehazi were more than happy to accept the invitation. They were tired, hot, and very hungry.

After eating a satisfying meal along with the enjoyment of great fellowship they continued on their journey. Over the next several months she would notice whenever they were passing through Shunem on their way to wherever they were going and would invite them to participate in their meal. Each time Elisha and Gehazi gratefully accepted. Finally, this Shunammite woman told them to just stop in for a meal whenever they were passing through. They happily and gratefully took her up on the invitation.

This woman knew that Elisha was a true man of God, and her heart was drawn to the God whom he served. One day she approached her husband, "I know that Elisha is a holy man. Let's make an upper room for him. In it we can put a bed, a table, a chair, and a lamp stand. What do you think?" He gladly agreed.

The next time the two men were passing through and stopped in for a meal she approached them with the offer, to which they readily agreed. It was delightful to be taken up the steps to the upper room; and sure enough, there was a bed, a table, a chair, and a lamp stand. In fact, the room was large enough for both men and with room to spare. Elisha felt an inner contentment in being cared for. It felt like a special love gift from God, straight through this kind man and his wife, and straight to his physical needs.

Early one afternoon Elisha lay on his bed enjoying a soft breeze flowing gently through the window. He was perplexed. He thought about all the meals this lady had fed him and Gehazi, as he gazed about this beautiful, comfortable room which they had provided. But what had he done special for them? Nothing!

Elisha looked over at Gehazi resting comfortably. His eyes were closed but Elisha could tell he was not asleep. "Gehazi," Elisha said, "wake up." His servant's eyes flew upon. "I would like you to do something for me."

"Yes sir, what can I do for you?"

"I would like for you to find the Shunammite woman and bring her to me. I have a message I would like you to deliver."

Gehazi sprang to his feet and was out the door. In a few minutes he arrived back in the room with the panting, puzzled woman following close behind.

Elisha looked directly at Ghazi and said, "tell this lady we appreciate her kindness. I would like to know what we could do for her. Could we put in a good word to the king for her, or to the general of the army? We need to reciprocate her kindness."

Gehazi turned toward the lady and delivered the message. She responded with a smile. "No, I am perfectly content. I don't have need of anything. I live a good life among my own people and don't need any favors from any government officials." With that she turned and went back down the steps to begin preparation for the next meal.

Elisha was still not satisfied. When Gehazi returned to the room Elisha asked, "do you know of anything we can do to express our thanks?"

Gehazi didn't even have to think. "I know

one thing she needs. She has no children. Her husband is quite a bit older than she is and when he is gone, she will have no children to help her. She will be alone."

Elisha laid on his back thinking and praying. Finally, he asked Gehazi to call her back up to the room. This time Elisha talked directly to the woman. "Next year at this time you shall have a son."

She stood there stunned, at first speechless. Finally, when she could find her voice she said with a little chuckle, "that's not even possible. My husband is old. Don't lie to me, please. I don't want to be disappointed. But a year later, at that very time, this lady who had been so kind to them did give birth to a tiny baby boy, just as Elisha had predicted.

❊ ❊ ❊

Several years sped by as Elisha's ministry continued to flourish and grow. During these years the Shunammite's baby grew into a little boy. One particularly hot morning he asked his mother if he could go into the field to see his father. She was very busy and happy for him to go. He dashed out of the house toward the field where his father was busy harvesting. But by the time he reached the harvesters the child was crying in agony because his head was pounding with pain.

Alarmed, the father called one of his servant's over to carry the child back to his mother who dropped all her responsibilities to take her little boy onto her lap where she cuddled him, rocking, trying to sooth the pain away. Eventually he became listless and gave a little shudder. And with that, the child ceased to breathe. He was dead.

Horror swept over the mother. This was her promised son, the heart of her heart. Trembling, she stood to her feet and did the only thing that came to her mind. She climbed the steps to Elisha's upper room, laid her small little boy on the bed, shut the door, then hurried out to see her husband and asked for one of the young men to saddle up a donkey. She needed to see Elisha, she mentioned to her husband, not adding that the child was dead. She assured him that everything was well, and she would be back before too long. Mt. Carmel was a distance of about twenty-five miles, and there was no time to lose. She told her servant to hurry as fast as the donkey would go.

Elisha happened to be rather absently

gazing down the road when he noticed the rapidly approaching animal and cart and was immediately alarmed. "Ghazi!", he called, "Something is wrong. Hurry and meet the lady from Shunem. Ask her if everything is all right. Is her husband well? Is the child well?"

Ghazi rushed down the road and as he approached, she called out assuring him all was well. She knew she could not afford to waste a moment of time. As the exhausted donkey approached close to Elisha she was out of the cart and on the ground holding onto his feet.

"Oh, man of God," she now sobbed. "I beg you come quickly to my house. My son just died. I have placed him on your bed. I know your God can give him his life back."

Ghazi was much younger than Elisha, so Elisha handed his servant his staff and told him, "hurry on ahead and place this on the face of the child. We'll follow behind." Ghazi headed toward Shunem and the other two followed pulled by a very tired donkey.

Ghazi rushed into the yard of the house, raced up the stairs, and just as they had been told, there lay the boy. His skin was waxy and he was not breathing. Reverently, he placed the staff on the face of the child just as Elisha had instructed. But nothing happened.

Agitated, Ghazi rushed outdoors to wait for Elisha's arrival. "I did exactly as you asked," he breathlessly said. "But nothing happened. The boy is indeed dead. I'm afraid it's too late."

Elisha only shook his head and along with Ghazi, hurried into the house and found the child on his bed. They closed the door. Grief stricken; Elisha called out to the Lord for guidance. He then laid down on top of the child and breathed into his mouth. Nothing. No response. Elisha paced. Ghazi paced. Elisha continued his desperate prayer. Once again Elisha laid his own body on the body of the child: eyes to eyes, hands to hands, mouth to mouth, breathing his own breath into the lungs of the little boy. Then he felt it: a slight movement under his body. The child sneezed, not once, but seven times. The movement increased and Elisha was by now on his knees beside the bed: Tears flowing, thanking and praising the God of Israel for this mighty miracle. Finally he whispered to his servant, "Call his mother to come up here. Her son is very much alive."

Within minutes, she was up the stairs, and on her knees, tears flowing in gratitude and praise.

Then she stood up and reaching down in awe and mother love, picked up her small son into her arms and held him lovingly against her as she turned to go back down the steps and into their house.

THE MIGHTY GOD OF MIRACLES

After the amazing miracle of life having been restored to the lifeless child in Shunam, Elisha strongly felt the need to return to his students in Gilgal. It had been too long, he felt, and was concerned as to their well-being. He and Gehazi returned briefly to Mt. Carmel then set out the approximate eighty miles toward Gilgal.

It was about a four-day trip for the two men. The closer they drew to Gilgal, the more obvious it became that the area was in a state of famine. When they had located their students, it was clear this group of one hundred men had not been getting quite enough to eat. Elisha couldn't help but notice that the men gathered around him seemed to be having trouble concentrating. Yes, they were clearly hungry, so it probably needed to become the first item of business to be addressed.

Elisha turned to Gehazi and said, "find a large pot, put it on the fire and mix up a batch of stew." With that announcement every man was on his feet scattering to find something to throw into the stew pot.

One of the younger men ventured into a field to gather herbs where he noticed a wild vine with gourds growing on it. This enterprising young man gathered all he could carry, took them to their meeting place and set to work slicing those gourds and throwing them into the bubbling pot of stew.

After a while, Gehazi sniffed, noticing the stew had a somewhat earthy Oder to it; but, he shrugged, reasoning it probably would taste just fine. As soon as the stew was considered done, the men enthusiastically dug in... but only for the first bite. First one man called out in alarm, then the others joined in. "It's poison! This stew is poisonous! It's going to kill us," all the while spitting out mouthfuls of the vile tasting concoction.

Instantly, Elisha had the solution. "Quick! Find some flour! In a few minutes someone handed him some flour which he threw into the pot. After stirring the pot of foul tasting stew, Elisha tasted it. Then said, "Everyone eat up. It's safe and it tastes wonderful." Gingerly everyone ladled some onto their plates, took a bite or two, and immediately returned for more. No one went hungry.

But God wasn't finished yet with his miracle of grace. The next day a cart arrived full to the top with all kinds of good foods. These foods were a tithe of the first fruits of this man's harvest. That which he had first harvested was now being offered to Elisha as the man's tithe. This wonderful gift included several different types of grains, and twenty loaves of barley bread.

"Gehazi," Elisha looked to his servant. I would like you to take this bread and feed the men.

Gehazi looked panic stricken at Elisha. There are one hundred men here. I can't feed them with only twenty loaves of bread! It's not possible."

"Just do it," was Elisha's reply. "It will be enough, and there will be plenty left over." And it happened just as God had promised.

* * *

Naaman awakened to an odd sensation. Something wasn't right. It wasn't that he was in pain. In fact, it wasn't even quite wrong. But what was it? He couldn't really say. Something just wasn't... well.... Something was just different.

Naaman, was an important man in the Syrian army, one of the King Ben Hadad's favorite leaders, a man highly valued. He was a man of great prestige exercising great authority. Naaman was the commander of the Syrian army, a general; the number two man in the nation.

What was troubling Naaman was a whitish patch on his skin. It was scaly, stiff, hard to the touch, a very dry patch of... what? He feared what it could be. It was a terrifying symptom of the dreaded disease leprosy. Fortunately, for now anyway, the dreaded patch was well hidden under his clothing. What was he to do?

This morning Naaman couldn't linger too long in his preparations of the day. The spot was hidden by his uniform so that gave him time to monitor it. Maybe it would go away on its' own.

As of this moment, he had a meeting to attend and army troops waiting to be inspected. A quick breakfast and then out the door.

But monitoring the awful spot wasn't working out the way he had hoped. The patch only grew. Nodules began to appear on his torso. Adding to his fear, the entire area of this growing nightmare was numb. There was no pain, no itching, just the awful realization that he, Naaman, Commander of the Syrian army, was a leper; just like all the other lepers driven from their homes into isolated areas outside the city walls. Naaman was a doomed man!

✻ ✻ ✻

She missed her home. But Naaman and his wife were kind to her, He may be the commander of the Syrian army. And his men may have captured her from her home in Israel. But they treated her well and she was content. And now Naaman had admitted that he had leprosy. It made her feel very badly. Not only was he a kind man, but what would happen to her if he were to be banished from his position and driven out of the city to die?

Mara thought of the two prophets back in

Israel who had brought about so many miracles during their years of ministry. First, there had been Elijah. Elijah had died, but now there was another great prophet in Israel. And Mara couldn't get it out of her mind. If Naaman were to go to Israel and see Elisha, wouldn't Elisha heal him of his leprosy? She had no doubt that Elisha's God could heal Naaman… but would he since Naaman was the commander of the Syrian army… and the Syrian army made raids on Israel? But the more she thought about it, the more she was convinced that he would do it.

It was with some hesitation and fear that the young Israelite maid, Mara, finally stood trembling before her mistress and simply declared, "If only my master would see the prophet who is in Israel, he would heal him of his leprosy."

* * *

The day came only too soon when Naaman requested a private meeting with the king and was forced to admit the awful enemy that had taken control of his body. "Oh King, Ben Hadad, I have awful news. I'm afraid I am a leper…" He couldn't finish the thought as he waited dreading the awful pronouncement that he would have to leave the palace, the city, his position and report to the leper community outside the city walls. The terror of his future was so hideous, that he was unable to stop his trembling.

King Ben Hadad was quiet for an awful moment as he digested the shocking news. Into the quiet Naaman added," but there is a young girl in my house who was captured in a raid by my men. She mentioned to my wife that there is a prophet in Israel who can heal leprosy."

King Ben Hadad's face brightened, and he said, "I'll write a letter to the king of Israel. Get prepared to leave as soon as possible." So that the prophet would certainly heal him of his leprosy Naaman gathered up a dizzying array of gifts: seven hundred and fifty pounds of silver, one hundred and fifty pounds of gold. Added to the spread of gifts were many costly garments. Surely such a delivery would ensure his healing.

After the trip preparation, Naaman appeared once again before the king and was handed a letter he was to offer to King Joram, king of Israel. The letter did not go over well. "Now be advised, when this letter comes to you, that I have sent Naaman my servant to you, that you may heal him of leprosy." The reaction was one of consternation and rage.

King Joram tore his clothes and raged, "Who does King Ben Hadad think I am? Does he think I am God and can kill and then raise that person from the dead? No, certainly not, so why would he send a man to me to heal that person from leprosy?"

The enraged King Joram was at the point of a war declaration when Elisha received the news and said, "Why have you torn your clothes? Why this reaction? Send this man to me and he shall know there is a God in Israel."

A greatly relieved Naaman took his horses and chariot to where Elisha lived in Samaria and arrived at the prophet's door., desperately in need for the God of Israel to intervene in his life. But to his dismay, the great prophet, Elisha did not come to the door. Instead, he sent his servant, Gehazi. This rubbed the great Naaman the wrong way. Naaman was accustomed to royal treatment. After all, hadn't he brought gifts only offered to royalty? However, the wise and godly prophet knew Naaman needed to be humbled.

Gehai relayed Elisha's instructions to

Naaman. "You are to go to the Jordan River and dip seven times, and you will be healed."

Had Naaman heard right? Dip into the muddy Jordan River; not once, but seven times? A slow burn filled his chest. He had already traveled a hundred miles. The prophet Elisha had not even tried to appear to see him at court. Then, when he arrived at Elisha's house, a servant had been dispatched to meet him, and now he is being told to travel about another thirty miles, only to dip in the muddy river; not once, but seven times? Unconscionable! If he was forced to go under water seven times, at least the waters of Damascus were clean.

With a roar of frustration and rage Naaman turned his chariot around to leave this cursed land.of Israel where he had been treated so rudely.

But Naaman had some servants who greatly respected their master and who wanted to see him healed. "Sir," they said, "If the prophet had asked you do a difficult thing, wouldn't you have done it? This is a simple thing. Please do it!"

Naaman looked at them quietly, studying their anguished faces. Finally he nodded his head and turned into the direction of the Jordan River. When they approached the river and he looked at the waters, it was even muddier than he had anticipated. With a sigh and a shake of his head he removed his clothes and waded into the cold, muddy waters. He dipped once, twice, three times. Coming up he studied his skin. The leprosy was still clinging to him. From the shore he heard, "The prophet said seven times! Don't stop now!"

Four... five... six..., another examination showed that nothing had happened. He was still a leper. And then he dipped one more time... the seventh dip. When he emerged from the water a mighty cheer erupted from his servants. Naaman's skin was healthy and free of the dreaded disease. Tears fell freely. It was a holy moment. Naaman bowed his head in a great emotion of thanksgiving.

✿ ✿ ✿

It was thirty-two miles back to Samaria. A humbled, grateful Naaman once again appeared at Elisha's door. This time Elisha received him. "Now I know," Naaman humbly stated. there is no God in all the earth except the God of Israel. He is now my God. Now please, I have some gifts I brought to you. Please accept them."

But Elisha shook his head "no". "I cannot accept your gifts. I am not the one who healed you. God healed you. Now go in peace."

Naaman stood silently in front of Elisha and then asked, "Let your servant be given two mule loads of earth to be taken back to Syria, upon which I may worship. I can no longer offer sacrifices or burnt offerings to the false gods of Syria. But may the Lord pardon me when I must go and help my master when he worships and bows down in the temple of Rimmon, and I must incline my head.

❋ ❋ ❋

Naaman departed with Elisha's blessing. Standing in the background was Gehazi who had heard the entire exchange between his mentor, Elisha and Naaman. Gehazi served Elisha as Elisha had once served Elijah, preparing for the day when Elisha was also taken away from this earth. But unlike his master, Ghazi's heart was greedy and Naaman's offer of gifts penetrated his heart. The more his mind pondered the offer, the more monstrous the greedy desire grew.

After Naaman had gone a short distance

from the house, Gehazi raced after the chariot, calling out for them to stop. Naaman stepped out of his chariot and anxiously asked if anything was wrong.

After catching his breath, Gehazi said, "Yes, everything is well. However, two young prophets have just arrived who are in a desperate need. My master sent me to ask for a talent of silver for each of them and two changes of clothes."

"Oh, certainly," Naaman responded. "Here, take two talents of silver in two bags along with two changes of garments," and handed them to two of his servants who carried them a ways. Ghazi then took them and stored them in the house where he thought they would never be found by Elisha.

But Gehazi forgot one important piece of information. Elisha's faithful God revealed what Gehazi had just done. A sad prophet met his servant at the door of the house and asked, "Where did you go?"

Gehazi stammered and stuttered then shook his shoulders and mumbled, "nowhere."

Elisha said, "Yes, you did. Naaman turned the chariot around to meet you. You took silver and clothing. Because of that, the leprosy that had been on him will now cling to you and to your descendants forever." And with that, a shaken and shocked Gehazi turned to leave Elisha's presence, now covered in the dreaded disease of leprosy.

CAN IRON
REALLY FLOAT?

He watched sadly as his servant stumbled away from him, now covered with leprosy. Grief stricken; Elisha turned slowly to close the door of his home. Gehazi had made a devastating choice and must now bear the awful consequences of that choice. The prophet leaned against his door, his head lowered as he considered how sinful actions always begin first in the human heart; and when petted, begins to take root, and will eventually spring up unawares out of the heart that's been allowed to harbor that temptation. It couldn't help but now explode into devastating action. Gehazi had demonstrated he could never follow Elisha's ministry, as Elisha had followed Elijah's.

But the ministry must go on. Tomorrow he had to leave to visit one of the several schools of prophets where he was overseer and spend time instructing the students. As Elijah had been, Elisha was also concerned that the next generation would know the Lord and understand his Word. Early the next morning Elisha was on his way. When he arrived at the school, he noticed the students were busy making some plans. "We're thinking," one of the young men explained to Elisha, "the place where we meet with you is very small and too crowded. We would like to go down to the Jordan River, each of us cut down some trees for poles, and build a large enough area for us to meet." Elisha nodded his approval, agreeing it was a good idea. Whenever he met with them, the students would study together, sitting before him, and they would eat together. In this case, the student body was expanding and now the area where they would meet for study and instruction was far too compact and uncomfortable.

Another student quickly added, "Would you come with us? We could use your input."

Together the men walked in the direction of the Jordan River. Upon reaching the river, the men fanned out searching for the trees best suited for the structure they were planning to build. Suddenly, a cry of pure agony split the air. "Master! Master! Oh no, This is terrible! What do I do?"

Elisha hurried to the spot of the cry and asked, "What's wrong? What happened?"

A frightened looking young man was pointing agitatedly toward the rushing waters of the Jordan. "It's the iron ax head. It's borrowed." He covered his face with his hands in frustration and fear. Any type of iron tool was precious and very scarce. He had borrowed this tool for the construction of this building. Now, this poor student would be forced to reimburse the lender.

"Tell me where it went in." Elisha watched as the frightened young man pointed to the area where it had flown up and out into the water. By now the entire school had gathered to watch the unfolding drama. Elisha picked up a stick and threw it into the river. To everyone's awe and amazement the iron head rose to the surface, floating on top of the water. The awestruck student bent over to retrieve the miracle, turning this into the best lesson of the day,. They had just witnessed a powerful demonstration of the miraculous power of the living God of Israel.

* * *

THE ALL
SEEING GOD

The idols may have had eyes but not a one of them could see. And certainly, the god Rimmon, the god of the Syrians and of King Ben Hadad, was no exception. That idol was as blind as any of the gods of any nation. It simply sat mute, deaf, and blind... a worthless piece of carved rock

Ben Hadad, king of Syria was a warring king who frequently sent his soldiers out on raids. And too frequently the nation of Israel fell victim to these raids. The Syrians would make raids into the border towns and take people, animals, crops... whatever or whomever they could snatch and then withdraw quickly. It was a frightening and unsettling way of life for the people of Israel.

One day King Ben Hadad decided it was time to make war on Israel and after consulting with his servants told them where to set up camp before the attack. However, the all-seeing God, Jehovah, was also in attendance at the meeting. He whispered the information to Elisha who appeared post haste to King Joram, king of Israel, cautioning him not to travel to a particular location because the army of Syria would be setting up a camp in preparation to make war on Israel. The king believed Elisha and promptly sent spies to check it out. Sure enough, Elisha was correct.

The Syrian King learned of this leak to his plans and erupted into a vicious rage. He ordered all his soldiers to gather and stand before him. They stood frightened and trembling before their master as he glowered at them one and all. Finally, he spoke through gritted teeth, and tight jaw, demanding to know who had been secretly betraying him and their own people by passing these secrets on to the enemy. Stunned, nobody could reply. Who, indeed, was the traitor? Finally, one brave officer spoke up. "Oh, King Ben Hadad, none of us has betrayed you. The prophet Elisha is the culprit. He hears every word you speak in your bed chamber and then tells them to the King of Israel."

This revelation only made the king even more infuriated. Now his rage was redirected to the infuriating prophet who lived in Israel. So, what if he had healed his general of leprosy! This prophet was to be hunted down and killed for his treachery.

After calling his troops together and preparing them to head toward Israel he was informed that Elisha could be found in Dothan, a small city just twelve miles north of the capital city of Samaria. The next day a large marauding army set out to bring in one man. The parade of soldiers included horses and chariots and foot soldiers. They approached Dothan and encircled it at night, ready to rush in shortly after daybreak.

Very early in the morning Elisha's servant, Ariel, was up and walked out the door of the house. Terrified, he rushed back in and shook Elisha awake. "Wake up," he babbled in fear. They're here. They're going to kill us. We're going to die! What are we going to do?" Ariel ended his frantic words on a crescendo of fear.

Elisha was out of bed trying to take this in. "Who's going to kill us?" He asked in a sleep state of puzzlement.

"Those men. That army that's ready to rush inside They're all around the city!"

Elisha led his frightened servant outside and prayed simply, "Lord, open this young man's eyes that he can see your army. And then he saw it: The hills were filled with horses and chariots of fire all around them. He stood in stupefied awe at the awesome army of the Lord, encamped all around them. There were far more in the Lord's army than those surrounding the city. Ariel's fears evaporated into a holy awe at the power of a Holy God who filled the hills and valleys and heavens all around him and his master Elisha.

The order was given, and the Syrian army began the advance into the city. Along with the first sound of marching Syrian boots Elisha prayed a simple prayer, "Lord, strike these men with blindness." Instantly, the soldiers began to flounder, not knowing where to go. As a vast confusion overtook these men Elisha located their commanders and said, "You have taken the wrong road and ended up in the wrong city. If you'll follow me, I will lead you to the man you have come to see." Elisha hadn't lied. He was no longer in Dothan and was now headed toward Samaria.

And he, their leader, was the man they had come to take prisoner.

All along the route toward the capital and palace of King Joram, the people of Israel watched in stunned amazement as their prophet, Elisha, accompanied by his young servant and apprentice, Ariel, led an entire meek marauding army along the road to Samaria. The soldiers... what was it that made them so meek and so... confused? Could it be that they were blinded? Their vision so clouded that they couldn't discern their surroundings.

Twelve miles of weary and confusing roads finally came to an end when Elisha halted his massive parade. King Joram, along with his officials quickly exited the palace with the commotion taking place outside. In amazement, the king noticed Elisha, and lined up behind him a very confused army of Syrian soldiers trying to discern their surroundings. Then he heard a booming prayer being offered up, "Lord, open the eyes of these men so they can see," and with that their eyes were fully opened, and it was with shock they saw that they were in Samaria and the man they had come to seize stood directly before them.

The astonished king burst into a rambling,

"Shall I kill them. Shall I kill them. Shall I kill them, my father?" (This term was an expression of total respect that he had for the prophet.) But Elisha shook his head "no". "Not, my king, you wouldn't kill men you had captured. Give them some food and water and then let them go back to their master." But King Joram did better than that. He set a feast before them.

The army returned to King Ben-Hadad. But Israel had won a major victory. The marauding bands of Syria not long raided the borders of Israel.

THE
TRUSTWORTHY
WORD OF
THE LORD

The troublesome Syrian border raids had ceased and the relieved people of Israel, along with their king, had relaxed and settled down to their day by day duties and activities. But they had forgotten one important detail. King Ben-Hadad was a warring king who thrived on sending his army out to make war on other nations. And according to his calculations it was time to go all out in battle against Samaria. In fact, he encircled the city of Samaria determined to starve them out. The walls were up. The gates were secured. But eventually the food was destined to run out and the people would face starvation... while the Syrian army simply waited it out.

However, there was another factor in this disaster: A very large factor! It was located in the unrepentant heart of King Joram, king of Israel. King Joram was guilty of following the wicked practices of his ancestors. He was a worshipper of Baal and participated in all the practices of that idolatrous and immoral worship, ignoring the commands of God and the frequent warnings of the prophets. They had forgotten the miracle of Mt. Carmel. And now, a severe judgement was about to befall the capital city of Samaria.

Day followed day within the besieged city. First, the flour began to run out. Their sources of meat such as chickens, sheep and cattle caught inside the walls were quickly butchered and eaten. No animal was safe from the table. Then followed the animals designated as unclean by God: such as; goats, donkeys, horses... even donkey's heads and the droppings of doves eaten as food and being sold at exorbitant prices. True starvation was now lurking within the homes of the people. And still the Syrians surrounded the city, eating, drinking, visiting, sleeping enjoying their camping experience... all the while hearing suffering taking place on the other side of the walls. And then the ultimate suffering and grief broke out...

* * *

The angry and desperate king couldn't sleep. Early one morning, shortly after the sun had risen in the sky, he left his exquisite ivory palace to take a walk on top of the thick city walls. As he slowly walked, he couldn't help but notice the decaying city below him. The shriek of a woman captured his attention. "Help! Help", she screamed up at him. "Oh, my lord, the king, please help me!" Her agony was heart wrenching, so much so that the king could not turn away.

"What's wrong", he called down to her. What's your problem?"

In pure agony she responded, "a woman told me yesterday that if we ate my son, then today we would eat her son. So we boiled my son and ate him yesterday. But today she has hidden her son."

The king was beyond stunned. This siege had now resulted in cannibalism. With a voice shaking in fury he finally responded, "today the head of Elisha shall be removed from his body. This is his fault!"

* * *

Elisha was sitting relaxed in his home, surrounded by the elders of the city. Normally the city elders would have gone to Joram for wisdom and counsel. Instead, they were visiting with Elisha, seeking his counsel and wisdom.

As Elisha and the elders were visiting, King Joram was standing on the city wall, appalled at how low the city had declined. In his rage he ripped his robe revealing the sackcloth he was wearing underneath the robe. However, this sackcloth wasn't being worn as a sign of repentance and seeking God's help. No, instead it was a sign revealing his anger towards the sovereign God whom he blamed for all his troubles.

Joram turned to his messenger ordering him to find the Prophet Elisha and have him executed immediately. But the king was so enraged that he followed after the messenger to make certain the job was done.

As the two men were hastening on their way to rid Samaria of this infuriating prophet, God was speaking to his beloved prophet. Elisha interrupted the verbal exchange and spoke to the men, "a messenger has been sent from the king, who is right behind the messenger. The king has ordered my execution, placing the blame of this siege upon me. When the messenger arrives, hold the door shut and don't let them in."

At that moment the knock sounded and the men stood against the door holding it securely closed. Coming through the door was the furious voice of the king. "This siege is all your fault! It's the fault of the Lord whom you serve and I will no longer wait for him to act. I'm taking charge now and will begin by ridding Israel of you."

Elisha responded by saying, "it's your own sin and the sins of the people that this has come upon you. But because of the mercies of the Lord you are blaming, he has this to say to you: "At about this time tomorrow food will become available, and the siege will end."

The officer with the king snorted in derision. "That's not possible! It can't rain provisions from the sky!"

"Oh but, it will happen," responded Elisha,

"you will see it with your eyes, but you will not eat of any of the miracle of provisions." A subdued king and his officers withdrew from Elisha's house, and the elders went to their homes encouraged.

* * *

As darkness fell over the city hungry stomachs and frightened inhabitants lay upon their beds dreading to face another day. But just at the entrance of the city gate, living in miserable isolation, four lepers sat talking with each other. One of them spoke up and said, "What are we doing here? If we enter the city, we'll die of starvation. If we continue to sit here, we'll die of hunger. What about surrendering to the Syrians? They may kill us, but maybe not. Maybe they will give us something to eat. What do you think?" They continued to sit in miserable silence. But finally, one of them spoke up and said, "Let's do it."

Unbeknownst to the four men the Syrians had been awakened at twilight hearing a frightening racket. Each man heard a huge approaching army The sound of horses, and marching men and the sound of approaching chariots. Screams and yells spread across the camp, "The King of Israel has hired the Hittites and the army of Egypt to attack us!' And they fled toward the Jordan River, scattering clothes, weapons, and other possessions along the way. In their panic they didn't want anything to slow them down.

Walking hesitantly into the camp the lepers were surprised at the silence of the camp; even more so to see the scattered articles of clothing, weapons, and other treasures on the ground and along the road. Where were the soldiers? Why was it so eerily quite and apparently deserted? Cautiously they approached one empty tent and then another. Hungry, they found stores of food. The four men ate until satisfied, then gathered up clothes and other valuable discarded items and hid them.

But after a bit they stopped and drew a conclusion that what they were doing was wrong. Just a short distance away an entire city was dying of starvation, so much so that they were even eating their young. "We can't ignore the suffering and keep all this to ourselves." And with that decided the men approached the guard at the city gate asking to see the king.

A short explanation of what they had found

and within minutes they were being ushered to the king's officials. They were astounded at what the men had to say, "... and when we walked into the camp we saw no humans, only tied horses and donkeys, food, tents, and all sorts of other belongings, but no human."

The king was roused from his sleep and grumpily declared, "it's all a trick. They're hiding in the fields waiting for us to open the gates and plunder their belongings and then they'll rush into the city and take us over."

But one wise soldier said, "Let's check this out. We have nothing to lose. Let us take five horses and several men and see if we can find them. So, the king granted them two chariots with horses and sent them out. Sure enough, the Syrians were gone.

As morning broke upon the city the news rapidly spread across the streets and into the homes of the desperate inhabitants. They crowded out of the gates and into the tents of the Syrian army. Wheat, barley was being sold for pre-siege prices. Other goods made it into the homes. There was plenty of food. There was one man who saw but was unable to eat of the bounty. It was the king's official who had scoffed at Elisha's prophecy that the next day would be the day of God's deliverance. He had been appointed to man the gate leading into the Syrian camp. The press of the crowds trampled him under feet. He had been trampled to death.

LIVING COURAGEOUS IN AN EVIL AGE

Elisha looked out over the barren landscape, his mind troubled and reflective over the many years of his ministry. Both the physical battles and the spiritual battles had been many and varied. He could have been a wealthy farmer, just like his parents. In fact, with their deaths he would have inherited all the land. Did he regret the choices he had made? He shook his head. No. Serving the Lord had resulted in many tumultuous years. But would he change anything? No! A thousand times no! The presence and the power of God who dwelled within, and through him never grew old. He felt he must be the most blessed of all men. But, as he turned and slowly walked back to his home, he realized how the years had taken their toll. He was growing old. Now, his mind turned toward the problems at hand. Both Judah and Israel were steeped in idolatrous practices. Compromise with the surrounding nations had resulted with the kings insisting on ignoring the God of his people, and instead taking up the worship of the idolatrous and immoral gods around them.

Ben-Hadad was sick. Elisha was instructed by God to head into Damascus where he was confronted by Hazel, one of the king's officers. Hazael had been sent by the king to ask a question. "King Ben-Hadad would like you to tell him if he will recover from this disease or if he will die."

Elisha hesitated for a bit and then answered, "tell your master that he will surely recover, but that he really will die."

Hazael turned to leave but turned back in consternation. Elisha was staring at him, with a look that made him squirm. "What's wrong" He asked. After an uncomfortable silence Elisha finally spoke, tears running freely down his face.

"I know the evil you will inflict upon the

children of Israel. You will set their strongholds on fire. You will kill the young men. You will dash children to death. And you will rip open pregnant women."

Hazel was incredulous. "Me? No! I wouldnt do that. I don't even have that kind of authority. Not me!"

"Oh, but you will," Elisha interjected. "Because the Lord has shown me you shall become king." Sadly, Elisha turned and walked away.

Hazael returned to the palace where the king asked, "What did the prophet say?"

"He said you will recover." But the next day Hazel entered the bed chamber of the king, wet a piece of cloth, smothered the king, and took over the throne.

❊ ❊ ❊

Jehoshaphat, king of Judah had been a godly king. His faith in the faithfulness of God had been unshakable. But, after his death, Jehoram, Jehoshaphat's son, occupied the throne of Judah. He married King Ahab's daughter, Athaliah. Then, to add further insult and wickedness to his rule, he introduced Baal worship to the people. But God knew exactly what was going on, and he had a plan.

Recklessly, Jehoram set out to kill each of his brothers. His father, King Jehoshaphat had given each brother a fortified city to rule. Jehoram did not want his brothers to oppose his policies of Baal worship. So an enemy nation attacked Judah. They took away Judah's treasures, Jehoram's wives and sons. But God wasn't yet finished bringing judgement upon Jehoram. He soon became very ill and eventually died. But with his death the people did not mourn and refused to bury him with the other kings of Judah.

But Jehoram's evil legacy lived on in the heart of his successor, Ahaziah, who also followed the practices of his father and his great-uncle Ahab.

When God has a plan he may wait a while, and when the time is right, he will fulfill it. He had faithfully warned both Judah and Israel over and over through his great prophets Elijah and Elisha. But because they had refused to repent and turn from their idolatry and the evil practices, God was about to bring judgement upon them.

Ahazial went to visit his uncle Joram, now

king of Israel in the city of Remoth Gilead. Both forces had combined there. Several miles away the prophet, Elisha summoned a young prophet and gave him a solemn instruction. Handing this young man a flask of oil Elisha instructed him to go to Ramath-Gilead. "Get ready. I have a job for you to do.. Take this flask of oil and go to Remoth Gilead. When you arrive look for Jehu, who is commander of the Israelite army. Be sure to take him into an inner room, away from everyone else. Then you are to pour this flask of oil onto his head and tell him, 'Thus says the Lord over Israel, I have anointed you king over Israel.' Then open the door and flee. Do not delay!'

When the young prophet arrived in the camp, he looked over the vast assemblage of the army for the commander. Spotting a group or captains, he noticed the commander. Approaching the commander he stated, "I have a message for you."

"For which one of us? asked the commander.

"For you," replied the prophet. "But I need to see you in private."

The commander, Jehu, led the way to an inner room where the prophet said, this is a message from the Lord. He poured the flask of oil over his head and said, "Thus says the Lord, I have anointed you to be king over Israel. You are to destroy the house of Ahab, all the males, both bond and free. In fulfillment of Elijah's prophecy, the dogs shall eat Jezebel on the plot of ground at Jezreel." With that, the prophet opened the door and fled as though there was an entire army chasing him.

A solemn Jehu returned to his men. One of the men asked, "Who was that crazy guy? What did he want?"

Jehu shrugged his shoulders and replied, "nothing important".

"You're lying," said the man. "Tell us what he wanted."

Jehu lowered his head and finally admitted, "he is a prophet who anointed me to be king over Israel."

After a breathtaking silence each man hurried to remove his garment and place it on the top step. Then they blew their trumpets shouting out, "Hail to the king! King of Israel!"

THE CLOSE OF ELISHA'S LIFE

A highly energetic Jehu rapidly set out to do the work assigned to him from the prophet. Ahab's family, including his grandson Joram, now the present king; as well as their past and present policies, had long been a thorn in Jehu's side. Now, in obedience to the assignment given him, Jehu set out with great gusto to carry it out.

First, he headed toward Samaria where King Joram had retreated to recover from his battle wounds against the Syrians. As Jehu rode furiously into Samaria to eliminate the king, messengers on horseback were sent out to inquire about the troops marching into their city. Jehu would slow down enough to reply "Everything's fine. Are you with me?" Each messenger fell into line behind him. By this time, it became obvious there was a conspiracy taking place. As Jehu and the army approached the palace King Joram went out in his chariot to meet him. Jehu drew his bow, shooting him between his shoulder blades. The arrow penetrated his heart. Death was instantaneous. Jehu turned and ordered his men to throw Joram's body into the field that had once belonged to Naboth; the vineyard that King Ahab and Jezebel had stolen and then had him murdered, to cover their crime.

King Ahaziah of Judah looked on with horror. He had come to spend time with his cousin, Joram who had been recovering from his injuries. In a panic He and his men fled back toward Judah; however, Jehu pursued him and killed him. Some of the men were assigned to take his body to Jerusalem where he was buried in the tombs of his fathers.

But Jehu was not finished with his pursuit of justice. There, in Jezreel wicked queen Jezebel was looking out her window at all the commotion. In her vanity she applied paint around her eyes, had her hair fixed just right, then returned to the window to watch the show. Jehu looked up at the window, calling out to two of the servants, "Are you on my side? If you are, throw her down." Immediately she was hoisted up and pushed through the window. Horses hoofs trampled her underfoot and there, just outside the palace wall, she bled to death. Just as the prophet Elijah had prophesied several years previously, the dogs devoured the evil Jezebel who had led the nation of Israel into Baal worship and the immoralities of idolatry.

Elijah had prophesied that a time would come when not one of Ahab's family would be left alive. And Jehu was still on the warpath to make sure it was completed; He sent a letter to the elders of Samaria where the seventy sons of Ahab lived. "If you are on my side," he said, "then kill them, put their heads in a basket and meet me at Jezreel tomorrow." The next day he met with the men of the city and said, "Not one word that the Lord spoke through the prophet Elijah shall fall to the ground." Then Jehu and his men entered the city and destroyed the rest of Ahab's family and all who were friends of theirs.

There was one more prophecy which must

be fulfilled: Jehu sent out a message to all the priests of Baal, and all the adherents instructing them to go to the temple of Baal for a solemn assembly. "Ahab was a great worshipper of Baal, but I will be a greater worshipper and have prepared a large sacrifice to the god. No one is to miss this assembly, or they will be killed"

On the day appointed all the priests were there. All the adherents were present. Vestments were brought out for the worshippers, sacrifices were made. But surrounding the temple were eighty men who had been instructed to not let one person escape. The doors had been closed and then Jehu destroyed all the worshippers of Baal, and broke down the entire temple of Baal until it was nothing but a refuse dump. Thus, Baal had been driven from the land.

❊ ❊ ❊

Baal had been destroyed over the land of Israel. But Judah was now under the reign of a wicked queen, Athaliah who destroyed all the royal heirs; except for one year old Joash, who was Ahaziah's son. Joash and his nurse had been stolen away by his aunt Jehosheba, who was also married to the priest

Jehoiada. They hid him in the temple for six years until the priest knew it was time to bring him out and have him crowned.

When the day arrived, all had been well prepared, the temple protected on all sides, the young prince protected. Finally, Trumpets sounded, the joyous announcement was made of "Long live the king!" The people cheered and clapped. The young prince wore a royal robe. The king's crown was placed on the head of seven-year-old Joash. In his hand he held a copy of the law to which he would be accountable to the King of the Universe. Athaliah hurried to the temple to see what all the commotion was about. Rage filled her as her eyes took in the coronation. Athaliah, began tearing her clothes screaming, "Treason! Treason!" The priest, Jehoiada demanded that she be removed from the temple and taken in through the horse carriage of the palace and there she was to be killed... all the while Athaliah was screaming "Treason!"

The godly priest, Jehoiada made a covenant between the Lord, the people, and the new king that they should be the Lord's people. Then seven-year-old Joash was taken to the palace and the people of Judah tore down the temple of Baal, the altars, destroyed the priest of Baal, and declared that the Lord would be their God.

* * *

The prophet Elisha had served God faithfully and tirelessly, throughout the many years of ministry. Just as his mentor, Elijah had fought for the soul of his nation, so Elisha had taken up the mantle for the soul of the nation. And now his life here on earth was winding down and he became very ill. Joash, king of Israel heard about Elisha's illness and hurried to see him. When he saw how ill Elisha really was tears ran down his face. Leaning over the old prophet he wept almost uncontrollably. Joash knew Elisha was leaving this earth and it was almost too much to bear. Throughout the years Elisha remained faithful to the king and to the people. As he sobbed out his grief he said over and over, "O my father, my father, the chariots of Israel and their horsemen." He recognized the power of Elijah and Elisha's God, when God had even sent a chariot to catch Elijah up into the air.

Much to the sorrow of Israel and Judah, Elisha died and his body buried. Several months later a marauding army from Moab invaded the land. One of the Moab soldiers was killed in battle and was buried in the tomb of Elisha. The moment the soldier's body touched Elisha's bones, life had been returned to him and he stood up.

Because they each learned the secret of prayer and had a total trust and confidence that God was real: believing in his power to meet every need; Elisha, just like Elijah, had been filled to the full of the power of the living God. This same God lives in our world today, desiring to impart wisdom, anointing, and empowerment to his people... for the soul of the nation.

NOTE FROM
THE AUTHOR

"Confess your sins to each other and pray for each other so that you may be healed. The earnest prayer of a righteous person has great power and beautiful results. Elijah was as human as we are, yet when he prayed earnestly that no rain would fall, none fell for the next three and a half years! Then he prayed for rain, and down it poured. The grass turned green, and the crops began to grow again (James 5:16-18 NLT).

In reading the accounts of these two men, Elijah and Elisha, I sat in awe at their daring, trust, and confidence in the God of power. What was it about these two men that set them apart? I wondered. It was in the pondering of my mind and then rereading the different stories spanning the years of their lives I think I finally understood. It was a deep, trusting relationship with God. When they prayed, dramatic things happened.

Buried deeply in Elijah's heart and then in Elisha's heart was a burning fire that was never quenched: It burned for the nation's soul. They must be brought back to the God of their forefathers. Sin, corruption, worship of false gods, and wicked leadership led to decay from within, eventually destroying them. Never in the history of mankind had God ever used two men, as he used Elijah and then Elisha.

But this begs the question: What about today? What about the culture in which we live? What about the soul of our nation... our cities... our families... our churches? What about our own soul? What about our own relationship with this powerful Living God?

God's eyes are roving throughout the earth today, as in the days of Elijah, Elisha, Isaiah, and Paul... men and women throughout the centuries have wondered, "Whom can I send? Who will go for me?

Consider Isaiah 6:1-8 NLT: "In the year King Uzziah died, I saw the Lord. He was sitting on a lofty throne, and the train of his robe filled the Temple. Hovering around him were mighty seraphim, each with six wings. With two wings, they covered their faces; with two, they covered their feet, and with the remaining two, they flew. In a great chorus, they sang, "Holy, holy, holy is the Lord Almighty! The whole earth is filled with his glory!!' The glorious singing shook the Temple's foundations, filling the sanctuary with smoke.

Then I said, "My destruction is sealed, for I am a sinful man and a member of a sinful race. Yet, I have seen the King, the Lord Almighty!"

Then, one of the seraphim flew over to the altar, and he picked up a burning coal with a pair of tongs. He touched my lips with it and said, "See., this coal has touched your lips. Now your guilt is removed, and your sins are forgiven."

Then I heard the Lord asking, "Whom should I

send as a messenger to my people? Who will go for us?"

And I said, "I'll go! Send me."

✻ ✻ ✻

ABOUT THE AUTHOR

Ardyce Miller-Templeman

Ardyce Miller-Templeman hails from the heartland, born and raised in a Nazarene parsonage in the serene landscapes of North Dakota. After completing her high school education in Fargo, North Dakota, she embarked on a transformative journey at Olivet Nazarene University. It was during these formative years that she encountered and eventually married Dr. Ron Miller, igniting a lifelong partnership dedicated to faith, ministry, and learning.

Their journey in the ministry led them to Hyde Park, VT, where they undertook a unique endeavor by acquiring a former governor's mansion. This establishment would become Freedom Ministries, a beacon of light established with a board and 501c3 status. Serving as both a training and counseling center, Freedom Ministries opened its doors to pastors and church leaders from diverse denominations, all seeking guidance and assistance. Following Dr. Ron Miller's passing in December 1994, Ardyce continued the ministry's legacy, furthering its reach and impact.

Relocating to Colorado Springs, CO, the heart of their mission thrived anew under Ardyce's stewardship. In her pursuit of knowledge and growth, she delved into Fuller Seminary classes, focusing on counseling and theology to enhance her ability to serve others. Her dedication was steadfast, and in 2002, she concluded her role as the director of Freedom Ministries to embark on a new path of service.

Ardyce, an ordained elder in the Church of the Nazarene, radiates wisdom and experience. Her voice has resonated across numerous denominations, where she has served as a speaker for ladies' retreats, conferences, and churches throughout the United States, Canada, and Mexico. Now in a well-deserved retirement, Ardyce continues to be an inspiration and a wellspring of spiritual insight.

Family is at the core of Ardyce's life, with four children, fifteen grandchildren, and three great-grandchildren forming a tapestry of love and connection. Her passion for storytelling and history led her to become the author of "To Finish the Course," a meticulously woven timeline that explores the lives of the Apostle Paul and early Christians against the backdrop of the Roman Empire. Her literary journey continues as she works on her upcoming book, "Whatever It Takes," an exploration of the lives and legacies of two of the most remarkable prophets in history: Elijah and Elisha.

Ardyce Miller-Templeman's life has been a testament to faith, resilience, and unwavering dedication to sharing the message of hope. Her journey from a North Dakota parsonage to a dynamic ministry and beyond stands as an inspiration for all who are privileged to hear her story.

BOOKS BY THIS AUTHOR

A Shepherd's War: Navigating Spiritual Battles In Ministry

Introducing "A Shepherd's War: Navigating Spiritual Battles in Ministry"

Step into the captivating world of ministry, where battles are not fought with physical weapons but with the unseen forces of darkness. In "A Shepherd's War," author Ardyce Miller-Templeman takes you on an inspiring journey through the heart-wrenching yet victorious tales of a life dedicated to the spiritual battlefield.

From assisting her father's pastoral work in North Dakota to the monumental shifts that led her alongside her husband's call to ministry, Ardyce Miller-Templeman immersed herself in the challenges and triumphs that define the lives of pastors and church leaders. The road wasn't easy, and the spiritual warfare was real, but every step paved the way for a deeper understanding of the battle behind the scenes.

The narrative unfolds with a unique perspective, chronicling the diverse experiences of ministry, from her husband's role as a Christian school principal to his life as an evangelist, traversing the landscapes of heartbreak and spiritual combat that pastors across North America face daily. Amidst the chaos and trauma, a vision emerged - a training and counseling center explicitly designed for pastors, a sanctuary where they could find solace and guidance in their spiritual struggles.

The book's core concerns Ardyce Miller-Templeman 's personal transformation as she takes on the mantle of leadership within Freedom Ministries International. The pages resonate with a profound sense of purpose as she recounts her time in the trenches, detailing the immense trials she faced personally and professionally during her tenure. A revelation was born through tears, prayers, and unyielding determination - found within the pages of II Chronicles 20.

In this ancient biblical account, King Jehoshaphat of Judah faced insurmountable odds, with three nations converging on his tiny country. With unwavering faith and a recognition of his reliance on the divine, King Jehoshaphat turned to righteous principles and the assurance that the army of heaven was leading the way. As Ardyce Miller-Templeman and her husband delved into this narrative, they gleaned invaluable insights into the enemy's tactics and discovered a wellspring of hope. This account offered a roadmap to overcoming the darkness that seeks to engulf churches and pastors, providing an inside look into the adversary's agenda and a pathway to victory.

"A Shepherd's War" is more than a memoir; it's a guidebook for those battling on the frontlines of ministry. Within its pages, you'll unearth the strategies and principles Ardyce Miller-Templeman and her husband Earl embraced in their pursuit of triumph over adversity. Through their stories, you'll learn that victory demands unwavering obedience, discipline, and a resolute commitment to God's Word.

This book is a must-read if you're a pastor, church leader, or someone seeking insight into the spiritual battles underpinning the ministry world. Ardyce Miller-Templeman 's honest, raw, and insightful narrative offers a beacon of light amidst the challenges, providing guidance, hope, and a renewed sense of purpose. Join her as she unfolds the pages of "A Shepherd's War," Let its wisdom equip you to face your battles with courage, faith, and the knowledge that victory is within reach.

CLICK THE BUY BUTTON ABOVE NOW for yourself or a pastor who needs help!

To Finish The Course: The Apostle Paul And The Early Christians In The

Roman World

This historical novel spans the reigns of the Roman Caesars Tiberius through Nero. It tells the story of the fledgling early church and how they were impacted by Roman law and rule. The apostle Paul traveled extensively throughout that world, visiting metropolitan cities, fearlessly taking the Gospel of Jesus Christ straight into the heart of pagan worship. He suffered hunger, stoning, prison, flogging, beating, being shipwrecked three times, and being in constant danger of bandits. Yet throughout all of these reverses, he courageously and fearlessly defended his message and his God-given calling. Interwoven throughout the pages of this story are two Roman soldiers, Marcos and Gaius, who walk the Jerusalem wall, observing from their Roman viewpoint all that is going on in the Jewish world. They observe the persecutions led by Saul and, later, the puzzling change in his life. Eventually, because of the impact a changed Paul has upon their lives, they come to know his Christ. This very real and human Paul, along with the electrifying, heart-stopping world in which he and the early church lived, is sure to keep the reader on edge, wondering what can happen next. Paul and this early church were willing to give everything, including their lives, for the truth of the good news that Christ had come to set up his kingdom in the heart of man.

Made in United States
North Haven, CT
13 December 2023

45678685R00114